SEMIOTEXT(E) INTERVENTION SERIES

© Maurizio Lazzarato, 2013. Published by arrangement with Agence litteraire Pierre Astier & Associés. This translation © 2015 by Semiotext(e)

Published by Semiotext(e)
PO BOX 629, South Pasadena, CA 91031
www.semiotexte.com

Thanks to John Ebert.

Design: Hedi El Kholti
Inside cover photograph: Kathryn Kenny

ISBN: 978-1-58435-163-4
Distributed by The MIT Press, Cambridge, Mass.
and London, England
Printed in the United States of America

10 9 8 7 6 5 4 3

Maurizio Lazzarato

Governing by Debt

Translated by Joshua David Jordan

semiotext(e)
intervention
series □ 17

Contents

Introductory Glossary

Austerity: "In one year alone the 500 richest people in France have become 25% richer. Their wealth has quadrupled over a decade and now makes up 16% of the country's gross national product. It also accounts for 10% of French financial patrimony; that is, a tenth of the country's wealth is in the hands of one-hundredth of the population" (*Le Monde*, July 11, 2013).

While the media, experts, and politicians continue their hymns to balanced budgets, finance has followed its first expropriation of social wealth in the 1980s with a second expropriation today. The peculiarity of the debt crisis is that its causes have been raised to the level of remedy. The vicious circle is the symptom, not of the incompetence of the oligarchical elites, but of their class cynicism. They are pursuing a specific political aim: to destroy the remaining resistance (wages, incomes, social services) to neoliberal logic.

Public debt: Public debt has reached record levels in every country that has enacted austerity measures. This means that the rents of creditors have also reached record levels.

Taxes: The principal weapon employed in the government of the indebted man is taxes. Taxation is not a means of redistribution that comes after production. Like money, taxes do not originate in the market but rather directly in politics.

When, as is the case during debt crises, money stops circulating both as an instrument of payment and as capital, when the market no longer assumes its functions of valuation, measurement, and resource allocation, taxation intercedes as the weapon of political governmentality. Taxes assure the continuity and reproduction of profit and rent that crises interrupt; they exert economic-disciplinary control over the population. They are the measure of how effective austerity policies are on the indebted man.

Growth: America is currently at a standstill. The engine is running but the car is not moving. It keeps running only because each day the Federal Reserve buys 85 billion Treasury securities and real-estate obligations and, since 2008, has kept the interest rate at zero.

Only heavy subsidies keep America out of recession. It is unable to pull the rest of the world out of the crisis for which the country itself is responsible.

The enormous amount of money injected each month by the Fed has only barely improved the employment numbers, which are in any case mostly made up of low-wage service-industry jobs and part-time work. The injections of cash reproduce the causes of the crisis, not only because they widen income gaps among the population, but also because they subsidize and in so doing reinforce the power of finance.

Although monetary policy has failed to jumpstart the economy and employment, it has nonetheless fed an economic boom in one, and only one, sector—finance—even at the risk of another financial bubble. The huge quantity of money made available to finance the economy first goes through the banks, which get rich in the process. Despite the anemic growth of other sectors of the economy, the financial markets have attained new records.

While everyone awaits the signs of economic growth, something else looms on the horizon. The primacy of rent; massive inequalities between employees and their employers; monstrous discrepancies in property ownership between the richest and the poorest (900 to 1 in France); social classes stuck perpetuating their same conditions; the end of social mobility, which was already dismal (especially in the United States, where the American dream is now no more than a dream)—all this looks less like capitalism than a variation on the Ancien Régime.

Crisis: When we speak here of crisis, we mean the crisis that began with the collapse of the American real-estate market in 2007. In reality, the definition is rather limited because the crisis has been ongoing since 1973. It is permanent, only its name and intensity have changed. Liberal governmentality is exercised by moving from economic crisis to climate crisis, to demographic crisis, to energy crisis, to food crisis, etc. Changing names merely changes the type of fear the crisis evokes. Crisis and fear constitute the inexorable features of neoliberal capitalist governmentality. We will not escape the crisis (at best it might change intensity) quite simply because crisis is the form of government of contemporary capitalism.

State capitalism: "Capitalism has never been liberal. It has always been state capitalism."[1] The sovereign debt crisis has left no room to doubt how right Deleuze was. Liberalism is only one of the possible subjectivations of state capitalism. Sovereignty and governmentality always function together, in concert.

Over the course of the crisis, neoliberals have not tried to govern as little as possible but to govern everything down to the last detail. They do not produce "freedom," they continually limit it. They do not unite the free market and the rule of law, they suspend what little democracy remains.

The liberal managers of the crisis have been all too happy to include a "maximum state" among the apparatuses of governmentality, which exercises its sovereignty solely over the population.

Governmentality: The crisis reveals the limits of one of Michel Foucault's most important concepts—governmentality—and obliges us to develop it further. To govern, according to Foucault, does not mean "subjugating, commanding, managing, ordering, normalizing." Neither physical force nor a set of prohibitions, nor even a body of norms or behaviors, governmentality incites the individual to establish an environment that forces him, through a "series of flexible, adaptable rules," to react in one way instead of another. The crisis has demonstrated that the techniques of governmentality impose, prohibit, regulate, direct, command, hierarchize, and normalize.

The "privatization" of governmentality requires us to consider non-state "biopolitical" apparatuses.

Since the 1920s, governance techniques have developed based on consumption. They are deployed through marketing, polling, television, Internet, social networking, and so on, which affect all aspects of life. These biopolitical apparatuses assure the valorization and production of subjectivity as well as police control.

Class struggle: Neoliberal capitalism imposes and governs an asymmetrical class struggle. There is only one class, reconstituted around finance, the power of credit money, and money as capital. While the number of workers in the world has increased considerably since the 1970s, they no longer make up a political class and never will again. The working class is no longer a class. Workers do indeed have an economic and sociological existence: they form the variable capital of the new capitalist accumulation. The ascendancy of the debtor-creditor relation has marginalized them politically once and for all. Finance and credit allow capital to stay continually on the offensive. In the capital-labor relation, what remains of the workers' movement is always on the defensive and regularly defeated.

No longer based in the factory, the new class composition that has emerged over the years is made up of a multiplicity of situations of employment, non-employment, occasional employment, and greater or lesser poverty. It is dispersed, fragmented, and precarious, far from finding the means to constitute a political "class" even if it represents the majority of the population.

Like the barbarians at the end of the Roman Empire, it makes incursions—as intense as they are short-lived—only to withdraw immediately afterward into its obscure "territories," above all into political parties and trade unions. It does not establish itself. It tests its strength (still too meager) and that of Empire (still too great) then retreats.

Finance: Journalists, economic experts, and politicians spend their time in a profusion of useless debates: *Is finance parasitic? Speculative? Productive?* The questions are pointless because finance (and the monetary and fiscal policies that go with it) is *the politics* of capital.

The creditor-debtor relation marks an extreme discontinuity in the history of capitalism. For the first time since the advent of capitalism, the capital-labor relation is not at the center of economic, social, and political life.

In thirty years of financialization, wages, once an independent variable of the system, have been transformed into an adjustment variable. They constantly decline while labor time and the flexibility demanded are always on the rise.

Transversality: What must be emphasized is less the economic power of finance and its technical innovations than that it functions as an apparatus of transversal governance, transversal to society and to the planet. Finance also operates transversally to production, to the political system, to welfare, and to consumption.

The sovereign debt crisis reinforces, intensifies, and radicalizes, accompanied with ever-increasing authoritarianism, the transversal techniques of government—because "we are all in debt."

Human capital (or the entrepreneur of the self): The crisis is not only economic, social, and political. It is also and above all a crisis of the neoliberal subjective model embodied by "human capital." The project of replacing the Fordist worker with the entrepreneur of the self, of transforming the individual into an individual enterprise that manages skills as economic resources to be capitalized, has collapsed in the subprime crisis.

From this perspective, the situation of rich countries and that of developing ones, instead of diverging (the stagnation and decline of the former versus the growth and progress of the latter), converge in the production of the same model of subjectivity, "human capital," which entails maximum "economic privatization" and maximum "subjective individualization." Conversely, social policies everywhere establish minimums (minimum wages, minimum income, minimum services) in order to force the entrepreneur of the self to enter into competition of all against all. There are other ways of reaching the same objective. In Germany, where no minimum wage exists, there are eight million poor workers.

Capitalist globalization boasts of having pulled millions of poor people out of the profound misery of developing countries. In reality, the policies of globalization are not incompatible with neo-liberalism. On the contrary, even when they are carried out on a large scale, as in Brazil, they represent experiments designed to provide a labor force appropriate to the capitalism of developing countries.

Among the many causes of the protests in Brazil in the spring of 2013, one thing must be remembered. The minority now freed from poverty and the new urban-class composition now subject to impoverishment are confronted not only with a macroeconomy organized on the most classical neoliberal principles, but also with a two-tier welfare state: on the one hand, mediocre social services ("minimum services"), on the other, good schools, a working healthcare system, good-quality, if costly, social services. To access any of this, one must throw oneself into the free-for-all of "socialist" social Darwinism. Well-aware of the situation, the protesters fought for "social justice" and against developing countries' version of human capital. If the process is reversed in Europe, where "free" social services are being dismantled, the results are nonetheless the same. The construction of a two-tier welfare state has accelerated with the debt crisis.

Reformism: In neoliberal capitalism, any kind of New Deal that might lead us out of the financial crisis is impossible. The only reformism capital has ever undertaken occurred during the Depression, when real changes were introduced exactly contrary to neoliberal "reforms." The New Deal neutralized finance (what Keynes called the "euthanasia of the rentier"), redistributed revenue via consumption and social services, and challenged—tentatively, of course—the status of private property. Through politics it imposed the primacy of the capital-labor relation by striking a compromise with the workers' movement, which gave its blessing to the changes in exchange for employment and social services indexed to employment. It built a "capital of subjectivity" represented by the full-time wage-earner, something that today no government on the planet is doing or would do because it under-mines finance. Even the most recent left-wing government experiments in Latin America are far, very far, from achieving actual reforms of capital. It is obviously not their fault alone. It is rather that power relations capable of imposing anything whatsoever on financialized capital simply do not exist.

The revolts in Brazil struggled to remind everyone of precisely this state of affairs, first of all to remind the leaders of the workers' party (Partido dos Trabalhadores) but also those in Europe who have put their money into the experiments of "left-wing" governments in Latin America (and elsewhere).

The refusal of work: The cycles of struggles that began in 2008 and have spread as much in the "South" as in the "North" of the planet have attacked globalization in a more specific and less "ideological" way than the protests in Seattle (2001). They express a refusal of political and trade-union "representation," self-organization, the use of what one hypocritically calls social networks, which many blithely confuse with political organizing.

But once the spontaneity of revolt has passed, "What is to be done"? Are ideas and practices lacking? While it may be risky, we shall advance several hypotheses even if, for the moment, they must necessarily remain abstract.

Understanding political action as a kind of rupture, an event, can open new perspectives on the forms of expression and organization of contemporary movements, revealing what remained unthought during the revolutions of the nineteenth and twentieth centuries.

The formidable mobilization of the urban "labor force" in this new cycle of struggles (in Brazil, Turkey, Greece, Spain, Egypt) also and at the same time represents a general demobilization, a "refusal of work" directed at contemporary valorization, just as worker strikes were actions whose motivation was radical *désoeuvrement*, the stoppage, the immobilization, of production. The workers' *movement* existed only because the strike was a *non-movement*, a suspension of the roles, functions, and hierarchies of the division of labor.

Problematizing a single aspect of the struggle— "movement"—proved a major obstacle because it made the workers' movement a catalyst of productivism and industrialization and turned workers into eulogists of work, of the "scientistic" faith in the neutrality of "science" and technique. The other dimension of the struggle, the "refusal of work," was either ignored (except by Operaism) or insufficiently problematized by post-Operaism, which simply abandoned it.

The communist political imagination did manage to produce *The Right to Be Lazy*, a polemic written by Marx's son-in-law Paul Lafargue against Louis Blanc's *The Right to Work*. Yet it was read as a mere pamphlet designed to *épater les bourgeois*. The communists failed to see the ontological and political implications of the refusal of work, of the suspension of activity and control, and the possibilities these created for moving beyond the model of *homo faber*, beyond the arrogance of producers and the promethean promise of mastery over nature.

Rupture: In every political event numerous lines of development necessarily intersect, lines that may unite or conflict and work against each other.

A line (of self-interest) invested in current power relations, in established significations and domination, and a line (of desire and possibility) that suspends power relations, neutralizes dominant meanings, and refuses the functions and roles of control and obedience inherent in the social division of labor—a line that creates a new block of possibilities.

The line of movement has causes, pursues goals, and seeks to open a predictable, calculable, and probable space. The line of non-mobilization suspends the laws of capital, engages in a non-calculable, unpredictable, and uncertain process. Félix Guattari thought this could only be achieved by way of an "aesthetic paradigm," because subjectivity and institutions remain to be constructed according to a completely different logic from that of labor and manufacturing.

A political event does not at first change the world or society, it simply reverses the way of conceiving subjectivity and opens the way from one mode of existence to another. The rupture of the event is only a first step, a beginning, whose fulfilment remains indeterminate, improbable, or even "impossible" with respect to the principles of established power.

Obviously, a political struggle can only articulate the two moments of the event, passing continually from one to the other (from the possible to its actualization and vice versa). But to develop, to take on consistency, the line of non-movement, the refusal of work, remains strategic and must transform established interests and institutions. Rupture emerges from history and, out of the non-historic, untimely moment of rupture,[2] it must return to history in order to transform power relations and subjectivity.

This twofold, more or less heterogeneous dynamic, the existence and relations of these two lines, constitutes *the* problem of contemporary political organization. The possibilities created by the rupture the event inaugurates are the political stakes over which the political battle for their actualization and neutralization is fought. What one calls "betrayal," "co-option," and "reformism" do not enter in afterward. Alternatives are present from the start of the struggle. Reducing the line of creation of possibilities and their actualization to the line of established power relations, separating the line of movement from the line of non-movement and playing the one off the other—that is the goal of capitalist institutions and of the political and trade-union "left."

Institution/subversion: The two lines of political action created by the event-rupture follow different paths.

Recognizing current relations of force, the line of mobilization enters a dualism of power in order to undermine capitalist institutions. The dualisms of capital are not dialectical; they are real and must really be undone.

Without subverting the three "nomoi" (appropriation, distribution, production)—concepts I borrow from Carl Schmitt for their radicality, concision, and relevance in defining all political orders—developing the line of non-mobilization can only be illusory. Without the expropriation of expropriators ("appropriating" not only the immense wealth captured through financialization and austerity, but also expropriated knowledge and existential territories), without a radical challenge to appropriative individualism ("distribution"), without subverting the concept of "production," starting from the very source of action, *désoeuvrement*, it is impossible to begin processes of a new type.

Recognizing the possibilities created, the line of demobilization seeks to proliferate the multiplicity of processes of subjectivation (and their institutions), processes that are not only political but also existential and non-totalizable, according to the necessities of the first line of struggle against the logic of capital. The forms of expression, struggle, and organization are not the same in the two cases. Hence the difficulty of thinking what comes after the "riots," for neither the party nor the trade union is capable of thinking and holding together this new, twofold dynamic.

Representation: The refusal of representation is deeply anchored in the new class composition. The conditions of contemporary political action make such a refusal necessary.

Political representation presupposes the identity of the represented, whereas the line of demobilization suspends precisely these established "identities."

Representation implies functions and roles that establish hierarchies and inequalities. The refusal of work suspends these hierarchies and inequalities and affirms equality, moving beyond a society divided into forms of self-interest.

Representation closes the rupture that the creation of possibilities opens by reducing developing subjectivities and institutions to established identities and power relations. This is why political movements currently disappear so quickly from public space. The conditions for assuring their political autonomy have yet to be invented.

The possible: Contrary to the economistic definitions of capital (cognitive, cultural, immaterial, etc.), Guattari calls his economy an economy of possibles. Capitalism (and its power) is above all defined as absolute control over what is possible and what is impossible. The first watchword of neoliberalism has been "there is no alternative," in other words, there are no other possibles than those proclaimed by the market and finance. In the midst of the sovereign debt crisis comes the same refrain: the indebted man must pay because no other possibilities exist. What is expropriated by credit/debt is not only wealth, knowledge, and the "future," but more fundamentally the possible.

Desire neither strictly refers to libido nor simply to urges but to the possible (Deleuze/Guattari). There is desire when, out of a rupture in past equilibriums, relations emerge which had previously been impossible. Desire can always be identified by the impossible it eliminates and by the new possibilities it creates. Desire is the fact that, where the world was once closed, a *process* secreting other systems of reference breaks through.

Signs and machines: Machines are everywhere except in critical theory. They form a kind of "constant social capital" essentially composed of computers and digital machines. Signs are the semiotic engines of these machines; they constitute the asignifying "language" through which machines communicate among themselves, with other non-humans, and with humans.

Signs and machines form enormous networks which are at once apparatuses of valorization, of the production of subjectivity, and of police control. The transversality of finance is effective only because machines and signs function transversally throughout all of society.

Signs and miniaturized digital machines also traverse matter, bodies, and objects, which are now animate not only metaphorically, as in the Marxian theory of the fetish, but also in reality, for they perceive, receive, and transmit information.

Capital is a social relation but it cannot be reduced to intersubjectivity. Relations are first of all machinic, in other words, composed of humans and of an ever-increasing number of non-humans. Capital is a social machine from which technical machines derive.

Capital is a semiotic operator: Capital is a semiotic and not a linguistic operator. The difference is considerable: in capitalism, sign flows (money, logarithms, diagrams, equations) act directly on material flows, bypassing signification, reference, and denotation, all of which are linguistic categories incapable of accounting for the operations of the capitalist machine.

Asignifying semiotics (money, logarithms, etc.) function whether or not they signify something for someone. They are not caught in the dualism of signifier and signified. They are operative signs, "power signs," that do not involve consciousness or representation (diagrammatic activities). Capitalism is machinocentric and not logocentric.

Force: To even begin to secure that which might emerge from the event-rupture, to discover for ourselves new forms of macropolitical organization, a final and fundamental condition must be met: the ability to block capitalist valorization, the possibility of establishing power relations and maintaining them, of opening spaces of power over time. In an asymmetrical class struggle, it does no good to play ambassador or diplomat. Capital can do without mediators; because nothing poses a threat, it has no reason to make peace. Power relations are too favorable. It can do pretty much whatever it likes.

Class struggle is conducted in a specific way, and with all the necessary violence, solely by the class that has been recomposed around financialization. The real is still dominated by the "laws" of capital, the most formidable of which is the introduction of the infinite into production and consumption.

It is impossible to define a new politics without an analysis of capital, on the one hand, and, on the other, without a practice of struggle and a practice for utilizing counterpower.

1

PROFIT, RENT, TAXES:

THREE APPARATUSES OF CAPTURE

> *"Schoolmaster: Tell me, my child, where did all this wealth*
> *come from? You could not have acquired it all by yourself.*
> *"Child: It comes from papa.*
> *"Schoolmaster: And papa, where did he acquire it?*
> *"Child: From grand-papa.*
> *"Schoolmaster: But of course! How did it come to grand-*
> *papa?*
> *"Child: He took it."*
>
> —Goethe quoted by Marx in *Capital*, vol. 1[1]

What has become of the indebted man during the crisis? What has he been up to? The answer is quite simple: he has been paying. He must expiate his fault, his debt, by constantly paying new taxes. But not only that.

A massive new appropriation/expropriation has been underway since 2007. The last one caused the current crisis; it began in the late 1970s and led to an unprecedented concentration of wealth. Today in the US, the quintessential country of neoliberalism, 1% of Americans hold 40% of the nation's wealth. In thirty years 99% of Americans saw their income rise by a mere 15% while the richest 1% saw theirs soar by 150%. The first economic appropriation was coupled with a no less unprecedented political expropriation of democracy. As the neo-Keynesian, and far from revolutionary, economist Joseph Stieglitz reminds us, neoliberals have finally succeeded in imposing a "government of the 1%, for the 1%, by the 1%."

To measure the scope (or excess) of neoliberal appropriation, one must look less at income, however, and more at patrimony. The magnitude is breathtaking. Let us take a French example this time. According to the Institut national de la statistique et des études économiques,[2] in 2009 those with incomes in the top 10% enjoyed a standard of living on average 6.7 times higher than the poorest 10%. If, on the other hand, we consider patrimony, in 2010 the richest 10% held a patrimony on average 920 times greater than the poorest 10%.

Major European and international capitalist institutions tell us that present economic circumstances demand the austerity policies that lie behind the second great expropriation. The latter simply allows state budgets to be put in order, after which we can start thinking about production and growth. Principally realized through taxation, the second appropriation is, in fact, strategic. How should these austerity policies, which are fundamentally fiscal policies, be understood? What role and what function do taxes play in capitalist strategy?

Every economic theory, whether orthodox or heterodox, would have us believe that appropriation is a function of "production," that wealth distribution depends on the contribution that "labor," "capital," and "savings" bring to production. In order to redistribute wealth, first we must produce; in order to take, first we must give. So says the common sense of economists, who await political solutions to the "social issues" of growth and increased productivity. Everything comes after production, even taxes and their distributive function.

Of course, the exact opposite is the case. Far from deriving from production or growth, appropriation and distribution antecede both. In capitalism, appropriation functions through a "three-headed" apparatus of capture: profit, rent, and taxation.[3] Their hierarchy and distribution change, however, according to the different phases of capitalist domination. If until the 1960s profit played a central role in appropriation relative to rent and taxation, the advent of neoliberalism reversed the relationship: expropriation from and control over the population was then primarily achieved through taxation and (financial) rent.

Following the private and sovereign debt crisis, the situation has again changed, and what has come to predominate is the capture apparatus of taxes. Capitalist government has been forced to change very rapidly the relationship and hierarchy of the three capture apparatuses, hence the recourse to "technocratic governments."

A preliminary redefinition of the concept of production

From the late 1970s to the early 1980s, neoliberalism made a decisive strategic shift, subordinating profit to the hegemony of financial rent and taxation. To understand the change, we must dispose of the economistic conception of "production."

The capitalist concept of production encompasses not only industrial capital and industrial capitalists, on the one hand, and, on the other, labor and workers. It also includes money and taxation as its actual and necessary conditions. Money and taxation precede and found both the market and the organization of labor.

Standard "economic science" reduces money to a mere specie currency capable of facilitating exchange and reduces taxation to an "unproductive" levy because both money and taxation originate in centers of power, generally those of the state; they do not derive from the market but on the contrary provide its basis and make it possible. This political, non-exchangist, non-productive, and non-economic origin, known since Antiquity, had to be erased to clear the way for the myth of the market's spontaneous coordination of economic agents.[4]

Money and taxation always depend on an apparatus of power (national states as well as transnational institutions like Europe or the banking or financial systems). They are at once apparatuses that initiate economic relations of power, assigning functions to everyone within the social division of labor, and apparatuses of capture that determine property rights.

It is insufficient to define what one calls post-Fordism by describing the changes in the organization of labor (cognitive or immaterial labor, just-in-time production, the role of innovation or knowledge, etc.). The transition from Fordism to neoliberalism presupposes no less, and perhaps more, important changes in how money and taxation function.

Even Fordism, the fulfilment of industrial capitalism, does not get its start in production but in money and taxation, which entail new modes of appropriation, distribution, and measurement. The Keynesian "euthanasia of the rentier" accomplished through fiscal and monetary policies and "nationalizations" differs little from a reformist confiscation (appropriation) of "rent." The regulation of money and taxation entails policies designed to neutralize rent and "rentiers" in order to promote "industrial capital" and employment. The relative sharing of gains in factory productivity and the creation of modest "social ownership" through the welfare state represent new norms of distribution determined above all by money and the tax system. "Production" properly speaking would continually reproduce and enlarge these "primitive" appropriations and distributions.

The transition to post-Fordism happened in the same way, by reversing the functions of money and taxation, which instead of neutralizing rent, increased it; by privatizing the issuance of money and thereby opening to the private sector everything the New Deal had, relatively speaking, socialized; by using taxation to transform the "nature" of welfare (massive income transfers to corporations and the rich, those of today's "new welfare class," while subpar social services are reserved for the rest of the population); by imposing new ("financial") measurements and new property rights (creditor capitalism, that is, a capitalism of stock and bond holders).

Does money come from taxes?

Perhaps still more than at the beginning of neo-liberalism, a moment when taxation nonetheless played a determining role, the crisis allows us to grasp the function of taxes and its complementary relationship with money. An analysis of the complementarity the crisis has made manifest can be found in *A Thousand Plateaus*.

If "money is always distributed by an apparatus of power,"[5] its circulation and turnover as well as the equivalence goods-services-money are assured through taxation, which makes money a general equivalent. "Taxes are what create money and taxes are what monetize the economy." Money does not originate in exchange or the market, as mainstream economic theory still believes, nor does it derive from labor. Money is integral not to commerce and labor, but to taxation, an instrument of power that is foreign to and independent of the market. In the economic circuit, taxes have played a fundamental role since Antiquity, as can be seen in the example of Ancient Greece. "[T]he tax on aristocrats and the distribution of money to the poor [were] a means of bringing money back to the rich,"[6] because the poor used money to purchase land and produce and in turn paid taxes on what they produced. The money borrowed came back to the rich "on the condition it not stop there, that everyone, rich and poor, pay a tax, the poor in goods and services, the rich in money, such that an equivalence money-goods and services was established."[7]

The same mechanism accounts for the capitalist response to the 1929 crash, as if with the New Deal Americans had discovered what the Greeks had known long ago, "that heavy taxes are good for business."[8] Taxes on aristocrats are akin to the expropriation of rent achieved in the Keynesian "euthanasia of the rentier" and the distribution of money to the poor akin to the income distribution assured by the welfare system. Everyone, rich and poor alike, pays high taxes (which today again has people going on about "extortion") but in order for money to find its way back to the "rich," thereby concluding the economic cycle and ensuring high profits.

Income distribution through wages, welfare, and high taxation did not inhibit "production"; indeed, the West has never seen growth rates as high and steady as during the postwar years. Rather, the political struggles of the 1960s and 70s chipped away at profits and forced capital to change its strategy by pushing for direct compensation and indirect social compensation to be considered independent variables. The need for another "economy," however, was always and uniquely political and not economic because growth, profits, and development are relations of power that precede economic relations.

The model of political economy (as well as the Marxism of Book One of *Capital*) must therefore be reversed. Barter does not come first, then exchange and money as means of equivalence, of circulation and payment, to finally end up at taxes exacted by the state apparatus of capture. Instead we must start with the political constitution of a stock of money; and now it is taxes and not exchange that create the equivalence of goods and services through which money is able to function. Given what has happened since 2007, it goes without saying that the capture apparatus of taxes rather than growth has monetized the crisis. Taxation assures the equivalence of goods and services which the market and money can no longer guarantee (the market collapses and money no longer circulates, especially among the banks).

By determining who must pay (certainly not those responsible for the crisis) and where the money must go (to the creditors and the banks responsible for the crisis), taxation ensures the wholly *political* reproduction of an "economy" which by itself would be incapable of functioning according to the fundamental political divisions that constitute it (creditors/debtors, capital/labor, etc.). The so-called "technocratic" management of the crisis, the government of "national salvation" (Greece), is quintessentially political. And its fundamental political instrument is taxation.

While taxes conserve rent and profit by guaranteeing their reproduction, in the short and medium term they do not lead to a new phase of production, growth, and accumulation. Debt reimbursement is not based on future wealth (new growth) but on current revenues. This is why debt is tantamount to a political levy.

Taxation does not ensure the monetization of broken institutions without at the same time providing the "measure" of the crisis. Taxation is the barometer of austerity policies, of the appropriation of the population's income, and of distribution among creditors, all which capitalism has maintained even during the crisis. Taxation measures less production than the power and control exercised over the population. In the final analysis, it measures the capacity of governments to impose austerity policies and the level of the population's acceptance of those policies.

Assuming its "sovereign" nature,[9] taxation installs an authoritarian government that suspends the already weak democratic system.

The capture apparatuses of the crisis

Fiscal appropriation can therefore be found not only at the beginning of the "financial" period but also within the crisis it has provoked.

The causes of the financial crisis do not lie in

the speculation and pathological greed of traders but in the fact that the capture apparatus of financial rents no longer ensures the appropriation of social surplus value or controls the relationship between distribution, exploitation, and domination that makes appropriation possible.

Sovereign debt would appear to be the origin and epicenter of the crisis. In fact, it is a mere consequence of the failure of American banks and of the transnational financial system. The root of the crisis does not lie in states' inability to pay back the debt they accumulated in bailing out the finance industry. The crisis resulted more fundamentally from the interruption of capitalist valorization and from the collapse of the accumulation derived from credit (the subprime crisis). Two news stories reveal the real reasons behind the crisis. First, the Reuter's headline (July 2012): "Tax Havens: Super-rich 'hiding' at least $21 trillion." The article goes on to say that the total is closer to $32 trillion, which comes to more than half of the world's total debt. We are expropriated so that creditors can be reimbursed and the money (ours) channeled directly into tax havens.

Still more illuminating were the details provided by *Le Monde* (August 2012): "Apple [with the world's highest market capitalization of $623 billion] holds more than $81 billion in offshore accounts, Microsoft $54 billion, Google $43 billion, and Cisco $42 billion." Here, too, the reasons for the crisis are clear: "They no longer know what to do with their war chests." The same situation is true of the other major multinational corporations listed on the stock market. They are sitting on a mountain of cash they have no idea where or how to invest. The accumulated capital no longer has a place or the means to increase in value. A security incapable of growth is degraded to an ordinary general equivalent, a means of payment. It can no longer control labor or society, in other words, it can no longer ensure new forms of exploitation/appropriation.

Capital can no longer "drain" society's productivity. Consequently, the task is turned over to taxation, which not only performs the functions of capture previously fulfilled by profit and rent, but also assures the cohesion of the three apparatuses of capture. Capitalism is inextricably a mode of production and a mode of predation. When predation can no longer be achieved through finance and production, a crisis erupts. The continuity of predation is from then on secured by taxation.

In all the European countries affected by the crisis, the tax machine has been vigorously engaged in order to effectuate the colossal transfers of money to the two immobilized apparatuses of profit and rent. Technocratic governments are first and foremost governments for and of taxation.

So-called "austerity" policies are in reality policies for multiple "forced" levies, running from taxes per se to cut backs in wages (reductions in nominal wages), decreases in welfare-state social spending (especially onerous cuts in pensions), and income deductions through price rises. Not the least "contribution," the latter is the result of "privatizations." To pay back debt, countries have auctioned off "public" property to the private sector.

French newspapers speak of a "tax beating" due to the 30 billion euros in new taxes announced by the socialist government in France. How should events in Greece, or in Spain, Portugal, or Italy, be understood, where tax increases greatly exceed the tax beating the French are supposed to take?[10] State intervention on the side of finance has further deepened inequalities (class differences), thus reproducing the true causes of the crisis.

The impossibility of reform (and an impossible New Deal)

During the crisis taxation has served both to destroy the forms of (constant and variable) capital that fail to conform to the logic of financial valorization and, from this destruction, to establish a possible new phase of accumulation. Historically, it is between these two movements that capitalism has waged war (in particular civil war) in order to reconfigure relations of power. In my opinion, what characterizes the current situation is the impossibility of enacting reform policies and, as a result, the central importance of destruction—especially that of the "social rights" and "labor laws" benefiting the labor force.

If newspapers, experts, and politicians are to be believed, everyone is at fault (workers, retirees, the unemployed, the sick, welfare beneficiaries, etc.), everyone except financiers and bankers. Are our elites blind or just cynical? The crisis has revealed a new and terrifying version of "groupthink" whose main consequence is the repression of the real. This is more than a subjective phenomenon; there are also "objective" reasons for the blindness and cynicism, namely that ending the crisis through a new New Deal has quite simply become impossible. Reform has become impossible. The elites cannot see the causes of the crisis, which are nonetheless right before their eyes, for "reforming" finance would mean calling capitalism itself into question. To a certain extent, they are driven to cynicism, a cynicism they complacently embrace.

Capital's reformist period represents a very minor parenthesis in the history of capitalism, lasting less than twenty-five years (from the Second World War to 1970). It was the corollary of a specific political conjuncture dominated by wars among states and civil wars, the rise of revolutionary movements, the fear of communism, and the depth of the economic and financial crisis of 1929.

Given this, reformism is now impossible because the potentially contradictory differences that still existed in the postwar period between industrial and financial capital, between the state and capital, between the institutions of the workers' movement and those of the state, between private and public property, between the representative system and capital, between the administrative state and capital, have disappeared. Initially Fordism but in particular neoliberalism imbricated the state (its administration and representative functions), finance, industry, private property, and so on, completely nullifying any kind of reformist option. Today, Keynesians' criticism of speculation and the stock market goes completely unheeded because finance is quite simply the driver of the economy and power.

The subjective production of the crisis

Taxes play a central role even from a subjective point of view because their basis lies in the expiation of the "fault" of indebtedness. When "public debt" is not honored, the fault is not rectified individually but collectively—through taxes. Taxation acts as a powerful vector for the transformation of each of us into the indebted man. Debt represents a mnemotechnics integral to the construction of a (bad) conscience and guilt. These are the subjective conditions necessary for keeping the "collective" promise of reimbursement, a promise state debts implicitly make.

The state, technocratic governments, and the media must therefore invest considerable energy to ensure a population's guilt for a debt into which it has never entered and, therefore, its responsibility for faults it has never committed. The laws, speeches, articles, and slogans deployed to this end are directly proportional to the scope of the fraud. During the crisis, technocratic governments have moved to construct a memory of debt not for individuals but for entire nations. The violence of taxes and appropriations is the privileged instrument, for only that which inflicts pain is engraved in memory, only that which hurts registers and remains inscribed in consciousness (Nietzsche).

The level of economic and discursive violence used by states, markets, and the media appears proportional to people's resistance to the creation of a memory of debt, proportional to their refusal to interiorize the sense of guilt, bad conscience, and responsibility.

Valuation and measurement

The rapid succession of capitalist phases (Keynesianism—Fordism/Neoliberalism—post-Fordism/

the latter's massive crisis) calls for several more general remarks.

The three apparatuses of capture represent three accounting machines that evaluate, measure, and allocate value and surplus value in a specific way. Each capture apparatus has its criteria for evaluation and comparison, its own measurements, and its own property regime, all of which coexists, while their hierarchy changes according to the political context. "Labor time" is one measurement available to the capitalist apparatus of capture. It was hegemonic when industrial capitalism dominated. Following this, measurement and appropriation were determined via financial rent and, since the crisis, they have been determined via taxation.

Taxes, rent, and profit function according to two complementary operations: evaluation/comparison, on the one hand, and monopolistic appropriation, on the other. Together, evaluation and appropriation define a property regime.

The capture apparatus of "profit" carries out the evaluation of "activities" to be "compared, linked, and subordinated to a common and homogeneous quantity called labor."[11] Yet labor does not preexist its capture apparatuses; it results from them. Labor and production do not come first, preceding their appropriation by capital. On the contrary, appropriation defines labor. The concept and reality of "labor" are established by capital.

> Labor and surplus labor are strictly the same thing;
> the first term is applied to the quantitative comparison of activities, the second the monopolistic appropriation of labor by the entrepreneur.[12]

The property regime of "profit" is the private ownership of the means of production held by the entrepreneur.

The neoliberal phase, on the other hand, is no longer founded on the valuation of "labor" but on the valuation of investment opportunities and the profitability of corporations. The new procedures for evaluation/comparison thus require new accounting rules that differ from those of "labor."

Return on Equity (ROE) is the "measurement" of a corporation's economic performance from the shareholder's point of view. We have gradually moved from a few percentage points of annual profit in the late 1980s to 10% then 15%. Today, a majority of French corporations with the highest market capitalizations show 20–25% profit margins. Appropriation is no longer handled by the entrepreneur but by the creditor. The hegemonic regime of property remains private, but it is now based on the ownership of capital securities.

The capture apparatus during the crisis is taxation. It introduces other forms of evaluation/comparison and, therefore, of measurement. Taxes assure the political comparison/valuation of assets and securities as well as appropriation, neither of which is guaranteed by the market.

The political dimension at the basis of the market became violently clear as soon as the "automation" of the market collapsed. In appearance, the property regime is no longer private but "public," because it is the state that collects taxes. In reality, it has become impossible to distinguish the state from capital and "public" property from "private" property since the state's tax revenues go directly to banks and to creditors' accounts hidden away in tax havens.

Carl Schmitt

Let us recapitulate. Production presupposes initial appropriation and distribution which, in the case of capitalism, occur in each new phase (Fordism, neoliberalism, the debt crisis). The apparatus of capture defines the conditions of production and distribution (growth) and not the opposite. This "truth" is expounded by an author very far removed from Marx, Deleuze, and Guattari—Carl Schmitt. Although it may seem strange to turn to Schmitt, as Marx recalled in his own time, it is often more useful to listen to reactionary thinkers than to seek out reformers.

It is easy to find critiques of economics among authors like Rancière, Badiou, and Agamben. The flaw in their theories, however, is the radical separation they establish between politics and economics based on an economistic conception of capitalism. It is less common to find a thinker like Schmitt for whom, in capitalism, *economics is politics*. Considered the prophet of the "autonomy of the political," he is, rather, the herald of its impossibility in postwar capitalism. Thus he transforms an adage dating from the German "Reformation," *cuius regio, eius religio*, into the startling new adage, "*cuius industria, eius regio*."[13]

Like Deleuze and Guattari, Schmitt helps us to avoid any kind of utilitarian, contractualist, or conventionalist conception of the economy. The economy always begins with barter, exchange, commodity capital, and the relationship between free contracting parties. The great merit of this reactionary thinker is to have reversed the order, replacing the market and exchangist starting point with a political one.

Following another path and employing other concepts, Schmitt critiques "liberal" thinking and its claim to neutralize the political nature of the economy by transforming it into "economics." From the lofty perspective of its scientific knowledge, economics asserts that the political solution to the "social question" depends on the growth of production and consumption, which can be understood and function only according to the laws of the market. Conversely, Schmitt argues that the economy is the contemporary form of the political such that the international division of labor represents the "true constitution of the earth today."

Every economic-political regime is constructed and organized on the basis of three principles which even capitalism cannot escape and which correspond to the three meanings of the word *nomos*. The Greek noun comes from the verb *nemein*, signifying, first of all, "to take." The German word *nehmen*, which Schmitt uses to create various neologisms, has the same linguistic root. In the first place, *nomos* means "capture," "conquest," in other words, "appropriation." Every new society (and every new phase of capitalist domination) begins with a capture, with a conquest, with what, according to Marx, might be called "primitive accumulation." Until capitalism, this phase consisted in the appropriation/expropriation of land as the foundation of every law and all economy. On the other hand, for twentieth-century capitalism Schmitt proposes the term *Industrienahme*, "industry-appropriation," as a translation of the first meaning of *nomos* under industrial capitalism.

> In place of the old right of plunder and of the primitive land-appropriations of pre-industrial times, [...] appropriation of the total means of

production [is substituted]: the great modern industry-appropriation (*Industrie-Nahme*).[14]

This method of conquest by industry differs from previous appropriations only in "being more intensively aggressive and of greater destructive potential in terms of the means of power utilized."[15] Only the possession of a large industrial space allows for the appropriation of global space and thus for the government of a world-economy.

The second meaning of *nomos* is "to distribute, to allot," in other words, "to divide." By designating "mine and yours," *nomos* defines ownership and the law. Appropriation, in turn, requires and enables measurement. The spoils of appropriation, what is acquired through conquest, discovery, and expropriation must be measured, counted, and divided. As in Deleuze and Guattari, evaluation/comparison and appropriation go hand in hand. They are the twin pincers of the apparatus of capture.

The concept of *nomos* originally meant a specific and concrete partition and repartition of land, but "If you ask me what the nomos of the earth is today, I can give you a clear answer: it is the division of the earth into industrially developed zones and less-developed zones." This is what makes up the actual "material" constitution of the earth.

The third meaning of *nomos* refers to "production" ("to pasture," "to manage," "to utilize," "to produce"). "This is the productive work that normally occurs with ownership. The commutative right of buying and selling in the market presupposes ownership as well as production deriving from the primary division: *divisio primaeva*. This third meaning of *nomos* derives from the type and means of production and manufacture of goods."[16] Schmitt's critique of exchange and the market is unequivocal.

The three concepts of *nomos* are contained in and encompassed by what is called economy, the sphere of differentiation which one would prefer remain distinct from politics.

In Schmitt's view, Lenin and Marx never quite surrendered to the sirens of production such as economists envision it. On the contrary, they sought the "political" foundations of capitalism in appropriation, expropriation, and property.

While Marx considers primitive accumulation and its appropriative violence as the necessary conditions to the birth and development of capitalism, Lenin sees in imperialism and colonization the only kind of appropriation capable of responding to the social question of the late-nineteenth and early-twentieth centuries. As for economists, they maintain that a solution can only be found in "production." The revolutionary changes in "production" presuppose for Marx, as for Lenin, "the expropriation of expropriators" and a new conception of the division of what is mine and what is yours, in other words, of ownership. And the same is also true, in a reformist mode, of the New Deal.

For Marx, revolution must address the three concepts of *nomos* in the same order Schmitt describes. "[Marx] concentrated the whole weight of his attack on the expropriation of expropriators, i.e., on the procedure of appropriation," "the great modern industry-appropriation." The expropriation of former owners "opens up new and enormous possibilities for appropriation," whether in terms of property or social function.[17] Today as in the past, expropriation and ownership are the political conditions for all social and political change.

Certain conclusions can be drawn from this. The concept of production must not be limited to productive factory labor. Nor is it sufficient, however, to extend the concept to social activity on the whole, for it at once encompasses and presupposes appropriation and division. The political cannot be defined as the organization of a kind of "living together" (*vivre-ensemble*) or as the establishment of a "common world" since both of these (the obsessions of the social sciences) are marked *ab initio* and in their very nature by a prior fundamental appropriation and division.

"Civil war" and the social state

Unlike economists or sociologists, Schmitt does not reduce the social state to the simple functions of redistribution and pacification of social ties. He makes the social state the sphere in which violent "civil war" manifests itself, a civil war whose latest chapter is being written by the debt crisis.

In today's crisis, liberals, under cover of reducing unproductive spending on public welfare, of eliminating bureaucratic obstacles to growth, are waging a decisive battle for the exclusive appropriation of the capture apparatus essential to the capitalist economy. Here too we must reverse the view of economists and recognize the political function of welfare.

According to Schmitt, in capitalism the problem of "appropriation" becomes pressing once the principal function of the state, the "mass social protections" provided by the social state, for example, consists in "distributing or redistributing the social product." However, "before a state of this type is able to distribute or redistribute the social product, it must appropriate it, whether through direct or indirect taxation, through the distribution of employment, monetary devaluation, or through other direct or indirect means. That being said, the positions of distributor and redistributor are in fact political positions,

positions of power that are themselves the object of appropriation and distribution. From this perspective as well, the question of appropriation remains crucial."[18]

At the end of the Second World War, Germany created a state—the social state—radically different from that which had exercised the violence necessary for "primitive accumulation" and even from that of the industrial revolution. The identification in the postwar period of the concept of the state with the "concept of the 'social' that all political parties in contemporary European democracies [...] adopted in some way"[19] is symptomatic of a profound change in the nature and exercise of sovereignty. The social state is a new kind of state that has little to do with the nation-state whose loss of autonomy led to its gradual but inevitable disappearance which Schmitt laments. Its functions and its forms of action would now be subordinated to economic logic: "The question is determined by the specific economic-industrial structure" of the state. The political and administrative systems of society must be "adequate to scientific, technical, and industrial development."[20]

The "state," the "social," the "economy"—terms among others that must always be understood as categories and realities traversed by class conflict. The social state thus becomes the "spoils" of a struggle among the forces that comprise the capitalist relation. This is how neoliberals understand the social state.[21]

Schmitt also calls the social state the total state. In his writing, the term does not refer to an all-powerful totalitarian state, it represents a symptom of the weakness, failure, and decadence of the state's old ethical and political principles. After 1945, Schmitt was no longer sure that the body of institutions being created in West Germany could still be called a "state," for it was being utterly transformed by the German constitutional process so as to conform to the "market." The process, which actually began with the birth of capitalism, would be intensified and accelerated first by neoliberalism then by the debt crisis.

Schmitt's remarks were prompted by the debate then taking place in Germany "not only about the social market economy, but also about the constitutional question with respect to the precise meaning of the federal social state and of the liberal social state prefigured in the Constitution of the German Federal Republic."[22]

Schmitt accuses proponents of the social state of minimizing the problem of "appropriation." Liberals and especially ordoliberals failed to recognize the political nature of appropriation and distribution (division), because they seemed to deny that one had to take from one group in order to give to another. Schmitt, on the other hand, sees looming behind the postwar state "an ethics of civil war" which the social state disguises as democracy and peace.[23]

Neoliberalism and the debt crisis have given us a brutal reminder of this political reality as low-intensity "civil war" has accelerated through increased taxes (from whom should new taxes be taken and how should they be imposed?) and spending (among whom and how should the revenue raised through appropriation be divvied up?). Since the New Deal, the social state has been the site of a conflict between political and social forces, for it is by way of the social state that those who give and those who take are determined.

In Carl Schmitt's postwar texts, we find the terms of a debate that took place as the social state was being founded, a debate at whose center were not only the concepts of the "social," "society," and "socialization," as Foucault shows in his lectures on *The Birth of Biopolitics*, but also the concepts of "appropriation," "ownership," and "distribution" as the preconditions of "production." The question of ownership, which is strikingly absent in Foucault's work on ordoliberalism, is at the heart of the debate, highlighting the concessions that capital had to make (unlike what happens today) in order to exit the crisis of 1929. The concessions affected what was most dear to capitalists—the rights of private property—and give an indication of the intensity of the power struggle waged by the revolutionary workers' movement at the end of the war. Hence the German jurist Hans Peter Ipsen's remarks in a speech quoted by Schmitt: "If the juridically indifferent concept of nationalization [...] were to acquire a meaning consistent with the historical and economic-political postulate of socialization, then it would demand the settlement of individual property ownership based on self-interest and subject only to general, public, and legal ties to property, at least through a surplus (plural-, joint-) ownership, by which *social groups that have hitherto been excluded from ownership will share it in the future.*"[24] This "settlement of individual property ownership" is especially apparent in the social state, in its public services and health "insurance" that cover old-age, unemployment, and so forth.

Neoliberalism took aim at the relative over-determination of "welfare" caused by workers' movement institutions and by the class demands institutionalized in social law and public services. It certainly did not oppose the capture apparatus of the state, its low productivity, or the growing drain it would have on the private economy. Indeed, the crisis has demonstrated the vigorous implication of the state apparatus.

The postwar social state enabled a new kind of distribution and, therefore, a new ownership regime, both in the service of state capitalism. Access to what Robert Castel calls "social property" was conditional because indexed to labor (or, better, to employment). This offered a means at once to recognize and to neutralize the political force of the workers' movement. Although the struggles and demands of the 1960s and 70s challenged this conditionality, once the strength of the workers' movement began to decline in the late 1970s, neoliberals had no reason to accept the "stranglehold" of the "unproductive" on social "plunder."

What liberals have had their sights on during the crisis is not a minimum state but a state freed from class struggle, from the pressure of social demands, and from the threat of expanding social rights. The debt crisis has clearly shown that the social state itself is at stake in appropriation, distribution, and production. The objective is not balanced budgets. The struggle has to do with the three concepts of *nomos*: "who" appropriates, "who" distributes, "who" utilizes social "plunder." The debt crisis is the political battle for the definitive seizure of the welfare state by neoliberal forces.

The crisis does not reveal a mere economic failure but rather a breakdown in the political relationship between appropriation, distribution, and production. Growth cannot pull us out of the crisis, only new principles of appropriation, ownership, and production can. Capitalists and neoliberals are incapable of envisioning what these principles might be, because now that reform has proved impossible the only thing they can do is implement populist and authoritarian policies.

An expanded concept of production

The non-economistic conception of production requires a final, fundamental development because production is also intrinsically "anti-production." This concept is perhaps Deleuze and Guattari's most important contribution to the definition of the nature of capital. It frees us from the admiration Marx still had for productivity and reveals capital's "demented," "destructive," and "irrational" side. The apparatus of capture, which in precapitalist societies transcended production (the aristocracy, the non-productive class, retained a portion of feudal production), has become immanent to it. At the same time as it produces wealth, capitalism necessarily produces misery and poverty. Necessarily, because in reality capitalism does not aim at producing wealth but *value*, value valorizing itself, profit producing more profit, infinitely.

This means that growth is a perverse solution to the social question and to the problem of justice, for growth is simultaneously production and destruction. Capable of producing only as long as there is private appropriation, capital can do no more than reproduce inequalities and the class differences that growth is supposed to resolve.

Production and anti-production are inextricable. They represent a Sisyphean task, an infinite ordeal, but one which, by continually reproducing the "scarcities" it is obliged to remedy, collides with the physical, biological, and material finitude of the world, the planet, and living beings.

Although capitalism is both a process of production and destruction, the crisis has led to the collapse of the former, on the one hand, and the "liberation" of the destructive side of capitalism, on the other. It is not a question of balanced budgets, of reviving the economy, but of destroying the constant and variable capital that fails to comply with the norms of valorization of the financialized economy.

It is now a given that capitalist deterritorialization is not relative but absolute. Deterritorialization not only means the destruction of the labor force, the destruction of productive capacities, techniques, commodities, modes of consumption deemed obsolete in order to create others which will in turn be destroyed in order to create still others. Deterritorialization also means the destruction of the earth, the planet, and the environment which make life possible. Capitalism has no territory of its own. It appropriates territories in order to exploit them and, once exploited, abandons them in order to appropriate and exploit others, which it will then abandon, and so on, ad infinitum.

With his concept of the "conquest of the earth," Schmitt accounts for only some of the consequences of this type of appropriation:

> world history [...] is the history of development in the objects, means, and forms of appropriation interpreted as progress. This development proceeds from the *land-appropriation* of nomadic and agrarian-feudal times to the *sea-appropriation* of the 16th and 19th century, over the *industry-appropriation* of the industrial-technical age and its distinction between developed and underdeveloped areas.[25]

Capital's appropriation of the earth is also intensive, because it exhausts the earth in the same way as it exhausts living beings and the environment. Capital treats the earth, matter, and the living beings that proliferate on the earth as exploitable "objects." Extensive appropriation (colonization, imperialism, the division of labor) is coupled with intensive appropriation (the exhaustion of natural resources, industrial and nuclear pollution, climate change, etc.).

Although Bruno Latour and Michel Serres have posed the question of ecology in striking ways, the first as "Gaia," the second as "Biogea," neither makes even passing mention of capital and the dynamics of capitalism. The "oversight" is all the more surprising because any claim to found a "new politics" must directly confront capitalism and its laws, laws which the crisis has imposed on all of us—even on philosophers. Capital has always contained in embryo not only the domination but also the current and potential destruction of the earth and of the nonhumans that inhabit it, both reduced to the status of appropriable and exploitable objects.

2

THE AMERICAN UNIVERSITY:
A MODEL OF THE DEBT SOCIETY

Man is no longer a man confined but a man in debt.
—Gilles Deleuze, *Negotiations*

This chapter takes as its starting point three statements by three intellectuals, the first a philosopher, the second an anthropologist, and the third an economist. All three maintain that money, exchange, and the market have freed us from the servitude of personal relationships, of which the paradigm is debt. The liberal and neoliberal freedom the market and money produce is, they claim, the freedom from debt, stating that if we are free, it is because we are no longer and will never again be in debt.

Let us take each author in turn. We will begin with the economist since the economy is, it appears, the origin of and serves as the model for all the social sciences.

Where does man's economic freedom come from—from the freedom of the market? From the ability that people have to free themselves from the debts into which they entered with feudal powers, from the personal debts they owed as vassal to suzerain or as serf to lord. Debt relief, which the widespread use of money made possible, freed people from personal bonds. Debt became transferable; it could circulate. This is the very essence of a monetary economy. Capitalism invented an egalitarian system in which ever-increasing numbers of individuals owe nothing to anyone. The market is, therefore, an extraordinary system for the abstraction, transferability, and liquidation of debt.[1]

Money frees us from the bonds of personal subordination because debt in the form of money makes relations impersonal, anonymous, and transferable. As we shall see, the terms "anonymous" and "transferable" have played a major role in the subprime crisis.

Let us now hear from the anthropologist. His study of archaic societies has taught him that historically debt precedes exchange:

We may ask if the whole of the enormous movement of the modern economy [...] might not be the last and most radical way to eliminate the gods, to do away with gift-giving and debt.[2]

The economy frees us therefore not only from economic debt but also from original debt, from primitive debt, from the "debt of life" owed to supernatural powers.

Finally, the philosopher concludes with an epiphany. He offers an apologia of the market and money then presents an extended definition of who we are. The modern individual, he says, is a sovereign individual, completely independent and freed of all bonds.

> In a non-monetary society, I can only claim a debt from relatives or friends for whom I have done something for free. On the other hand, when I provide a commercial (thus monetary) service, the person who benefits is, through his or her payment, immediately freed of all debt to me. The money he or she gives indeed constitutes a debt but to someone perfectly anonymous and abstract, to whom nothing binds me in terms of gratitude, recognition, or debt. Relieved of any kind of psychological or moral burden, exchange—at once rational, efficient, and free—develops very quickly.[3]

We learn to be free, then, not only in economic and religious terms but also in moral and psychological terms. With all these freedoms, we have finally become complete individuals.

These three intellectuals courageously advance a counterintuitive truth. It appears that until now we have been under the false impression that debt, far from disappearing, is omnipresent, especially given all the talk of private debt, sovereign debt, debt repayment, and the guilt of debtors that has invaded the media and has continued to influence our behavior over the last six years.

The production of knowledge is a financial enterprise

But before looking at the theoretical and political reasons that have led these thinkers to conclusions that everyday reality seems to contradict, I would like to focus for a moment on American universities, where two of the three men teach.

Why the university and why in the United States? Because this temple for the transmission and production of Western knowledge is also a model of the financial institution and, with it, of the debt economy. There are several reasons for this. On the one hand, the American university is the ideal realization of the creditor-debtor relationship. On the other hand, the American student perfectly embodies the condition of the indebted man by serving as paradigm for the conditions of subjectivation of the debt economy one finds throughout society.

A recent report from the New York Federal Reserve on US household debt presented data on

American student indebtedness. On March 31, 2012, the total amount students had borrowed and still owed in order to finance their university studies reached $904 billion, $30 billion more than just three months earlier. The number is equal to over half of the public debt of Italy and France. For much lower debt the European Union and the IMF promptly tore Greece apart, a country now in its sixth year of recession. For comparable or lower sums, recession, austerity measures, personal sacrifice, unemployment, and poverty are imposed on the millions of citizens of indebted countries.

In the US, two-thirds of university students graduate in debt. Today thirty-seven million people have gone into debt in order to complete their diploma. Students are indebted before entering the job market and stay indebted for life.[4] The Fed points out that, although home loans are still the primary source of household indebtedness, student loans are not far behind, having already surpassed credit card debt in 2010. With the economic crisis the unemployment rate among university graduates under twenty-four years old rose to more than 15%.[5] Many young graduates struggle to find a job as repaying their debt becomes less and less likely.

What better preparation for the logic of capital and its rules of profitability, productivity, and guilt than to go into debt? Isn't education through debt, engraving in bodies and minds the logic of creditors, the ideal initiation to the rites of capital?

Creditors and debtors

American students represent the ideal of financialized society. The social group is composed of a majority of debtors and a minority of rich creditors' children. In the production of knowledge, class division no longer depends on the opposition between capitalists and wage-earners but on that between debtors and creditors. It is the model the capitalist elites would like to apply to all of society.

To a university public composed of the indebted and the children of creditors, two of the thinkers previously cited teach that debt is finally in the process of disappearing thanks to money, trade, and the market. This kind of pedantic blindness to the obvious gives us a good idea of the state of the social sciences, bound, as they are, to the cultural hegemony of neoliberal universities.

Student indebtedness exemplifies neoliberalism's strategy since the 1970s: the substitution of social rights (the right to education, health care, retirement, etc.) for access to credit, in other words, for the right to contract debt. No more pooling of pensions, instead individual investment in pension funds; no pay raises, instead consumer credit; no universal insurance, individual insurance; no right to housing, home loans.[6] The individualization process established through social policies has brought about radical changes in the welfare state. Education spending, left entirely to students, frees up resources which the state quickly transfers to corporations and the wealthiest households, notably through lower taxes. The true welfare recipients are no longer the poor, the unemployed, the sick, unmarried women, and so on, but corporations and the rich.

The student debt bubble

Let us continue our tour of the factory of indebted students, the American university, so that we understand how contemporary capitalism functions.

In the US there has been talk of a student debt bubble comparable to that of subprimes, the risky mortgage loans whose collapse in 2007 plunged the US and the world into recession. Indeed, more than a third of student debt is "securitized," that is, grouped together then sold to investors in the form of derivative products. Contrary to what our three intellectuals claim, it is through securitization that the instruments of "freedom" from debt, the *transferability* and *anonymity* ensured by money, become the cause not of the disappearance but of the spread and proliferation of debt. The debt incurred to buy homes in the US, debt turned into negotiable securities—the famous subprimes—was in fact transferred to numerous banks and financial institutions. These transfers were precisely the vehicle for the infection and propagation of debt. Anonymity[7] further worsened the crisis when it became obvious that no one knew which banks held toxic assets and how many they had.

blinds people.

Financialization has fully established the "security societies" characterized, according to Foucault, by risk and freedom (characteristics which also define liberalism). Although continually confronted with the risk of time, that is, with the unpredictable and uncertain future value of credit/debt, financial institutions do not assume the risk and refuse all responsibility. Irresponsibility, in other words, the "freedom" from responsibility, is precisely what defines the behavior of financiers.

Thanks to actuarial techniques, they take risks of which they as quickly unburden themselves, by endlessly subdividing them, by making them anonymous, and by transferring them to other economic actors (a method also employed for student debt). When the risks undertaken are the source of an economic debacle (as in 2007), holders of "risk" transfer them, through the state, to the population. Finance and the state transform those who have taken no risks and therefore hold no responsibility into the responsible parties. The economic mechanism of crisis is always doubled by a subjective apparatus that reverses responsibility. It is hard to see why financiers, "free" to take risks without having to assume the consequences, would deprive themselves of such "freedom."

Control, subjectivity, time

Debt constitutes a new technique of power. The power to control and constrain debtors does not come from outside, as in disciplinary societies, but from debtors themselves.

Students contract their debts by their own volition; they then quite literally become accountable for their lives and, to put it in the terms of contemporary capitalism, they become their own managers. Factory workers, like primary school students, are controlled within an enclosed space (the factory walls) for a limited time and by people who, and apparatuses, which remain exterior to them and are easily recognizable. To resist, they might rely on their own resources, on those of other workers, or on the solidarity between them. Control through debt, however, is exercised within an open space and an unlimited time, that is, the space and time of life itself. The period of repayment runs to twenty, sometimes thirty, years, during which the debtor is supposed to manage his life, freely and autonomously, in view of reimbursement.

The question of time, of duration, is at the heart of debt. Not only labor time or "life time," but also time as possibility, as future. Debt bridges the present and the future, it anticipates and preempts the future. Students' debt mortgages at once their behavior, wages, and future income. This is the paradigm of liberal freedom, which is, as we have seen, freedom in name only. Credit produces a specific form of subjectivation. Debtors are alone, individually responsible to the banking system; they can count on no solidarity except, on occasion, on that of their families, which in turn risk going into debt. Debtors interiorize power relations instead of externalizing and combatting them. They feel ashamed and guilty. The only time that American students began to free themselves from the guilt and responsibility that afflicts them was perhaps, fleetingly, during the Occupy Wall Street movement: three months of revolt and thirty years of payback.

Debt is the technique most adequate to the production of neoliberalism's *homo economicus*. Students not only consider themselves human capital, which they must valorize through their own investments (the university loans they take out), but they also feel compelled to act, think, and behave as if they were individual businesses.[8] Debt requires an apprenticeship in certain behavior, accounting rules, and organizational principles traditionally implemented within a corporation on people who have not yet gone on the job market.

The credit relation in a magnetic strip

Our visit to American universities, for which our guide has been financialization, brings us to a form of debt very widespread in the US: credit cards. In 2008, 84% of American students had at least one credit card, versus only 76% in 2004. Still more surprising, students have on average 4.6 credit cards apiece. The explosion of university costs explains the upsurge in the number of credit cards.

The creditor-debtor relation is inscribed in their card's magnetic strip. Students carry it in their pocket just as they carry with them their relationship with finance. Every purchase is a financial act mobilizing credit and debt. The credit card opens the door to the consumer society and, by soliciting, encouraging, and facilitating purchases, draws the consumer/debtor into the vicious circle of stimulation and frustration. Debt is the condition and the consequence of the infinitely repeated act of consumption:

> Whereas consumer credit was given upon explicit request, the card system automatizes credit. The reversal of initiative is exemplary here: with credit cards, the credit relation is always already in

place; one need only use the card to activate it
[…]. We no longer apply for credit but accept
cards. The card payment system thus establishes
a structure of permanent debt.[9]

Debt as apparatus of capture

The interest payments debt demands are an apparatus for capturing and redistributing social wealth.
The capture of surplus value no longer occurs solely
through profit. In fact, the latter now represents
only a portion of rent. In finance capitalism debt
embodies the "vampire" Marx evoked to explain
how capital functions. It "sucks" social surplus value
and distributes it, severing the relationship between
labor and income, to the exclusive advantage of rentiers, which includes corporations. Everyone else is
condemned to forced labor, in other words, to pre-
carity or unemployment. With cuts in social
spending, drops in wages and income, we are all
paying for the damage creditors have caused. Not only
are we paying in their place but we have continued
to make them rich during and because of the crisis.

Debt functions in the university in the same
way it does everywhere else. Who benefits from the
interest students pay? First of all, the banks, who hold
the majority of loans and set interest rates at their
own discretion. Second, the federal government,
because its lending rates are much higher than

those at which it borrows money. And finally, university presidents, administrators, and professors (among which our intellectuals), whose salaries depend on the ever-growing indebtedness of their students who, in order to attend class, mortgage away their future paychecks.

I will conclude this first section with Aristotle's statement that "knowledge and money have no common measure." Throwing the assertion aside, finance has established an arbitrary as well as normative and effective measure. The debt incurred and the terms of repayment are the price to pay to access science and truth which, as everyone knows, are disinterested.

Money and debt

I would now like to present the theoretical foundations that have driven our three thinkers to such implausible conclusions. To that end, I shall focus on the monetary aspect of the question. For doesn't money, ever since the US went off the gold standard in 1971, constitute what one calls debt? And, in line with what Nietzsche writes in *On the Genealogy of Morals*, isn't debt "infinite debt" in contemporary capitalism?

Our three intellectuals express a doxa widely shared in the social sciences, namely that the market, exchange, and money free us from debt. Let us note to begin with that money poses formidable problems for an economic science that has shown itself incapable of integrating debt into its theories of equilibrium and growth. This fact makes dubious their ability to explain capitalism, which obviously represents not only a monetary economy but above all a credit-debt economy.

The money to which our three intellectuals attribute the capacity to free us from debt is commodity money, money as a means of payment, of measurement, and of accumulation. This exchange-money, as we might also call it, is one of the types of money in circulation, but in our capitalist societies it is not the one that plays a strategic role. Indeed, it is not money that embodies the power of capital. Capitalist money is money capital, credit money, debt money.

Exchange-money presupposes and establishes a symmetric (and contractual) relationship between producers and those that enter into exchange, whereas money capital establishes an asymmetrical relationship of exploitation, class difference, appropriation, and privatization. Marx said that on pieces of exchange-money the motto of the French Revolution was written—*liberté, égalité, fraternité*—but that on money capital other words could be read: domination, exploitation, the power of destruction/creation, debt, desire, predation, the prescription of other modes of production and distribution.

Against the rationality of commodity money,[10] which enables "*doux commerce*," supplants the violence of debt, transmits freedom, equality, and fraternity, rises the "irrational rationality" of money capital. Deleuze defines the latter in a way particularly suited to how the crisis has played out: "Capital, or money, has reached such a point of folly that there can only be one equivalent in psychiatry: what they call the terminal state."[11] Money capital reaches this terminal state, according to him, in the mechanism of the stock market, which "is perfectly rational […], you can understand it, learn how it works; capitalists know how to use it; it's completely mad, it's crazy."[12]

Deleuze and Guattari remind us in *Anti-Oedipus* that there is a difference in nature between the two moneys, one expressed by a difference in power. The authors go on to say that commodity money in all cases remains subordinate to money capital; to confuse them or make them synonymous is no less than a "cosmic swindle."[13] Worse still, to take only the first into account while ignoring the second, as our three thinkers do, is to add swindle to swindle.

The theory of debt of heterodox economics

Let us leave our three thinkers confined to their dead-end reasoning. Let us now turn to Michel

Aglietta and André Orléan's school of monetary regulation theory, for it introduces important innovations to standard economics. Here money is not deduced from barter first and market exchange second, as in classical or neoclassical political economy, but rather from debt. Unfortunately, this major shift is immediately undermined by a transcendent, holistic, totalizing conception of debt as a "life debt" exercising "collective" constraints on "individuals." Debt merges with human nature, defined as a "lack of being," a deficit, an incompleteness, which only the gods, the state, or society can remedy. As if to temper the audacity of defining money as debt, the proponents of the theory naturalize the latter through the concept of primitive debt and universalize it by claiming that debt is an archetype found in all archaic societies. Debt precedes exchange and, if Aglietta and Orléan are to be believed, it is always primordial debt, original debt, life debt, in other words, the "recognition of living beings' dependence on the powerful sovereigns, gods, and ancestors who granted them a portion of the cosmic force of which they are the source."[14] In exchange for the gift of vital power, the living are obligated to repay their debt, a repayment that has no end because, ultimately, the debt of life is an infinite debt. Debt functions in the same way as original sin.

Look around you: when you hear talk of "life debt," "original debt," and so on, you are bound to notice that the person speaking is a priest, a politician, or a psychoanalyst. The economist's entry into this exclusive circle is something completely new.

For these economists of regulation, life debt has another, particularly appealing function: it exercises and justifies sovereignty over the individual. "It constructs sovereignty and cements the community in its works and days, in particular through sacrifices, rituals, and offerings."[15] What heterodox economists seek is not so much the truth about how archaic societies function; rather, in original debt, in primordial debt, they seek the same holistic, transcendent, and restrictive debt they attribute to the state, to the social sphere, and to the collective in our societies.

The concept of life debt is presented in Deleuze, Guattari, and Nietzsche in a totally different way. It is neither a matter of nature nor of the universal. Original debt does not link individuals to the community; it is not the sign of a primitive indebtedness transmitted at birth, of an inaugural debt that no one can ever repay. On the contrary, it is "produced" by a definite political situation whose genealogy and history can be traced. Hierarchical, monotheistic, state societies institute the debt of existence, life debt, primordial debt, and turn it into infinite debt.

For our three thinkers, just as for the regulation school, archaic societies produce an inexhaustible debt, one which cannot be repaid, whereas in modern capitalist societies we are able to free ourselves from debt through monetary reimbursement. Deleuze and Guattari make the opposite argument: archaic societies are characterized by a "finite and mobile debt," while with the emergence of empires, states, and monotheistic religions, debt has become "infinite debt."[16]

> [T]he abolition of [small] debts or their accountable transformation initiates the duty of an interminable service to the state that subordinates all the primitive alliances to itself (the problem of debts). The infinite creditor and infinite credit have replaced the blocks of mobile and finite debts. There is always monotheism on the horizon of despotism: the debt becomes a *debt of existence*, a debt of existence of the subjects themselves.[17]

By introducing the infinite into the economy and production, capitalism preserves and extends the infinite debt of imperial state societies and the guilt, no less infinite, that monotheistic religions associate with debt. Finance capitalism has further intensified the process. It has placed finance and credit money at the heart of capitalist accumulation.

Debt is its driving force. It makes debt a promise one must honor in order to contract more debt without ever being able to stop the headlong advance. This is what the crisis makes clear with every morning news update.

The anthropology of sacrifice

This is not Orléan and Aglietta's first "abusive" universalizing operation. To find a non-economic foundation for money, they draw on suspect anthropologies that allow them to trace continuities between the transcendence of the sacred, of the state, of money, and of the social sphere.

By way of René Girard's anthropology and theory of sacrifice, they naturalize the political operation by which transcendence and mediation are constituted. Their primary genealogy of "money" is based on this theory of sacrifice, which anthropologists have never accepted due to the simple fact that, in its drive to universalization, it is quite plainly wrong. Sacrifice constitutes the transcendence relative to which everyone is indebted; it resolves the problem of "war of all against all" by revealing, through the sacrificial victim, a mediation, a transcendence (whose descendants are money, the state, and sovereignty), that pacifies the original violence that exchangers-producers perpetrate on one another.

Girard's Christian fundamentalism makes him confuse his desire for monotheism, centralization, and transcendence with the reality of most archaic societies. He thus turns "sacrifice" into a universal that is supposed to explain and encompass everything. His arguments betray a veritable mania for totalization.

> There is a unity that underlies not only all mythologies and rituals but the whole of human culture, and this unity of unities depends on a single mechanism, continually functioning because perpetually misunderstood—the mechanism that assures the community's spontaneous and unanimous outburst of opposition to the surrogate victim.[18]

Unfortunately, sacrifice is not in the least universal. It is not found in all archaic societies but only in those that settle the problem of power relations through transcendence. According to André Leroi-Gourhan, sacrifice was unknown in Paleolithic societies, nor is there any trace of it in hunter-gatherer societies. Other research confirms the non-universality of ritual sacrifice, giving the lie to Girard's hypothesis.

> The ethnological data are perfectly clear: from Oceania to the Americas, vast regions have never

practiced sacrifice. Never in Australia, New Guinea, Melanesia, or Alaska, almost nowhere in Canada, nowhere in the western US, never in the Amazonian lowlands, from the pampas to Patagonia and Tierra del Fuego.[19]

If, among the examples Girard cites, we examine the "cannibalism" of the Tupinamba Indians, the whole edifice of supposedly universal sacrifice collapses. Eduardo Viveiros de Castro has brilliantly shown that it is impossible to transform "Andean and Mesoamerican state formations, in which sacrifice is an essential theological-political mechanism,"[20] into a ritual common to all societies. Tupi cannibalism, for example, does not belong to this theological-political state order. It does not constitute sacrifice according to the criteria defined by Marcel Mauss because there is no "recipient," no "supernatural" forces, in short, no "sacred." In Tupinamba cannibalism the sacrificial arrangement of "sacrifier" (the one who offers the sacrifice), "recipient," and "officiant of sacrifice" simply does not apply.

The Amazonian shaman is both "officiant and vehicle of sacrifice," for instead of sending into other worlds "representatives in the form of victims, he himself is the victim [...]. We cross the threshold to another socioeconomic regime once the shaman becomes the sacrifier of others, once he becomes, for example, the executioner of human victims, the administrator of sacrifices offered by the powerful [...]. This is when we begin to see the shadow of the priest emerge from behind the figure of the shaman."[21]

The remarkable differences between Tupi cannibalism and the ritual of sacrifice have to do with two radically heterogeneous socio-cosmic orders, with the presence or absence of state mediation, its priests and bureaucracy. The institution of sacrifice does not proceed from human nature, from the original violence that supposedly defines all societies, as Girard would like us to think. It is instead the result of an appropriative political operation carried out by the state, the priest, and the bureaucrat as well as of the immanent practices of the shaman. To speak of sacrifice means that the constitution of transcendent political formations has already begun. Sacrifice and transcendence are born together; they in no way designate a primitive origin but rather a political victory over other forms of organization and other conceptions of the world and the cosmos. "The institution of sacrifice by so-called Andean and Mesoamerican 'high cultures' would mark the state's appropriation of shamanism, the end of the shaman's cosmological bricolage, the beginning of the priest's theological engineering."[22] We must recognize how new it is to see priests dressed up as economists.

The economists of money of the regulation school give to holism, transcendence, and the collective a pre-determined positive value because the latter are supposed to run contrary to the individualism of the market and of *homo economicus*, whereas in fact they constitute a centralizing, totalizing form of power no less oppressive than the individualism of the market. Just as Girard projects his monotheistic fundamentalism onto societies that were not monotheistic, so heterodox economic theory projects, through life debt, its need for state-institutional mediation onto societies organized in such a way as to avoid such mediation.

The *Genealogy of Morals* and "infinite" debt

Nietzsche and the *Genealogy of Morals* are directly— or indirectly by way of Deleuze's and Guattari's readings—at the basis of my own work on debt.

Anthropologists pass over the Second Essay because they believe that it fails to correspond to what their discipline has identified among archaic societies. Take, for example, David Graeber, who has recently written a lengthy book on debt.[23] According to him, Nietzsche accepted Adam Smith's argument that life is "exchange" and man a "rational being"; unlike the founder of political economy, Nietzsche is said to provide a picture of what the world would look like if interpreted in "commercial terms." Basing himself on Smith's thesis, Nietzsche does no more than corroborate the theory of original debt, primordial debt, and life debt we have already seen at work among heterodox economists.

Unlike the German philosopher, Graeber thinks that debt is merely exchange that has yet to come to an end, presupposing the equality of parties. Equality is suspended during repayment but it can be reestablished (and with it reciprocity[24]) once the debt is paid back. The anarchist Graeber, in unison with our intellectuals and political economists, believes that debt can always be reimbursed. Debt is a relation occurring against a backdrop of fundamental equality; it can always be honored and, in consequence, one can always "expiate" the attendant fault.

Our hypothesis says exactly the opposite. In capitalism, and particularly in finance capitalism, debt is infinite, unpayable, and inexpiable, except through political redemption, as Benjamin might say, and never through monetary reimbursement. How have we come to such diametrically opposed views? Nietzsche will help us rectify matters.

We shall very briefly focus on certain concepts that directly resonate with our current situation. First of all, *On the Genealogy of Morals* does not pretend to found an anthropology. It is an open polemic aimed at the exchangist, utilitarian

("What does utility matter!"), and contractual ("What do contracts matter!") conception of political economy and, on the other hand, at its theory of value and of the "rational man" that exchange is supposed to produce. Graeber, by making a claim that would make even an undergraduate think twice—namely that Adam Smith's *homo economicus* and its corresponding rationality are the basis of Nietzsche's philosophy—blithely mistakes the question of "value" with that of the value of the "market" and of political economy. Nietzschean man is indeed the "creature that measures values," that evaluates, the "valuating animal as such," but these values do not depend on the market or on *homo economicus*. It is neither the market nor *homo economicus* that creates, measures, and evaluates values. Values presuppose evaluations, "evaluating points of view," from which their value stems. As for evaluations, they are ways of being and modes of existence.

Against political economy, which had "appropriated" the category of "value" by deriving it from exchange, Nietzsche specifically opposes the future task of the philosopher: "the solution of the *problem of value*, the determination of the *order of rank among values*" and "the *value* of this or that table of values,"[25] "the *value* of existing evaluations." In order to critique economic and moral values, "*the value of these values themselves must first be called in question*."[26] We could not be further from the theories of Adam Smith.

Second, for Nietzsche, debt does not imply equality and reciprocity but their opposites. If credit/debt and not exchange represents the archetype of social organization, it is because the forces in play are not "equal" but asymmetrical. Credit mobilizes active and reactive forces (in relations between human beings as well as within each human being); it is the site where superior and inferior forces confront one another, the purpose of which is constructing a subjectivity "capable of promising." And promising presupposes a memory, a memory of words, which debt works to manufacture. Before the debtor-creditor relationship has any "economic" signification in the modern sense of the term, it expresses the process of breeding and shaping subjectivity. For Deleuze and Guattari, the logic of debt in archaic societies has nothing to do with exchange, because "the socius is inscriptive: not exchanging but marking bodies,"[27] "circulating—exchanging—[is] a secondary activity."[28]

Third, the *Genealogy* addresses the question of time, which, as Bergson explained, is nothing if not creation. Exchange is instantaneous whereas the specificity of debt is to include, to control, and to exploit time by actualizing the future. Debt is a promise of repayment and therefore concerns open and indeterminate time, the radical uncertainty of the future which the logic of probabilities cannot anticipate or control. Debt is the capitalist apparatus that closes and preempts time, mortgages its indeterminacy, strips it of all creativity and innovation, normalizes it. It is wrong to say that debt is an unfinished exchange, because duration, time, and incertitude constitute the specific difference with exchange. "To breed an animal *with the right to make promises*" means "to ordain the future in advance," "to stand security for [one's] *own future.*"[29]

Fourth, Nietzsche very clearly indicates the transition from finite and reimbursable debt to infinite and unpayable debt. The debt of life, original or primordial debt, is a relatively late invention first imposed by "the constraints of society," then by the state, and finally by monotheistic religions. The change "was not a gradual or voluntary one"; it was "a break, a leap, a compulsion, an ineluctable disaster."[30] Henceforth, people were accountable to society, the state, and the gods; active forces, which finite debt had to engage in order to act on reactive forces, were turned against the human being who would from then on be forever culpable. "[T]he *aim* now is to preclude pessimistically, once and for all, the prospect of a final discharge" "until at last the irremediable debt gives rise to the conception of irremediable penance, the idea that it cannot be discharged ('*eternal* punishment')."[31]

The creditor-debtor relation as the relation between active and reactive forces, as mastery over time, is preserved and extended by capital in the form of infinite debt. With finance capital, capitalism makes this relation the dominant one. In finance capitalism, it is impossible to pay off one's debt, since capital, like money, in other words, credit, is by definition debt. If one makes credit out of money, if one makes debt the alpha and the omega of capital valorization, reimbursement can never be achieved without destroying the capitalist relation. The creditor-debtor relation can never be settled because it assures both political domination and economic exploitation. To honor one's debts means escaping the creditor-debtor relation and this would mean exiting capitalism altogether. One can honor one's debts, but if one honors all of one's debts there is no longer any asymmetry, any power differential, no stronger or weaker forces—no more capital. Definitive repayment is, logically, the death of capitalism, for credit/debt embodies the class differential.

Because credit is the engine of social production, it must be systematically repaid and yet immediately and necessarily renewed, ad infinitum. Capitalism does not free us from debt, it chains us to it. It is not by bending to the injunctions of debt reimbursement that we will free ourselves. It is not through an act of repayment but through a political act, a refusal, that we will break the relation of domination of debt.

In conclusion, contrary to an opinion everyone from anarchists to neoliberals seems to share, the debt of today's capitalism is unpayable, unreimbursable, and infinite. The function of credit is expressed still more precisely in the literary, rather than economic, terms of Kafka. They apply particularly well to our condition as debtors, for, like Joseph K., we are all presumed guilty even if we have done nothing wrong. The form contemporary debt takes resembles at once an "apparent settlement" (we go from one debt to another, take out credit and repay it, and so on) and an "unlimited postponement"[32] in which one is continually indebted and the debt is never (and must never be) honored. Credit has not been given in order to be reimbursed but rather to be in continual flux.

This is not just the American consumer's situation; it is everyone's. Sovereign debt varies constantly while the "spread" informs us of the range of its fluctuations in real time. Variations in public debt in turn drive variations in wages, income, and social services, although always in the same direction—downward. Likewise, debt causes continual variations in taxes, but, likewise, always in the same direction—upward.

The debt reimbursement imposed on Europeans is therefore a political weapon employed to intensify and fulfill the neoliberal project: everyone knows that in both quantitative terms (excessively high amounts of debt) and qualitative terms (in finance capitalism debt is infinite) debt cannot be paid off. We must face up to this state of affairs and change it; we must change the sense of the unpayable by quite simply *not paying*.

I am often criticized for painting an overly bleak picture of the situation. To conclude as I began, I would like to respond with Deleuze's remark that "There is no need to fear or hope, but only to look for new weapons."[33]

3

CRITIQUE OF GOVERNMENTALITY I:
DOES LIBERAL GOVERNMENTALITY EXIST?
HAS IT EVER EXISTED?

Transformed into a crisis of sovereign debt, the financial crisis has imposed new forms of governmentality and new subjective models both on the side of those who govern ("technocratic governments") and on the side of the governed (the indebted man who expiates his fault through taxes). These new subjective models reveal the true nature of the techniques of governmentality and of the relationship between liberalism and capital better and more profoundly than was the case during the rise of neoliberalism.

Any critique of the liberal government of the crisis must confront Foucault's analyses. His lectures *Security, Territory, Population* and, in particular, *The Birth of Biopolitics* represent a considerable advance in the analysis of forms of control and government of populations. Foucault's work on liberal governmentality is integral to the development of his theory of power relations (from power as war and as strategy to power as "government"). Nonetheless, his understanding of the relationship between "capital and its logic" (to use his terms) and the state, as well as that between the state and liberalism, presents certain weaknesses. One might even say that the most striking limitation of his courses on governmentality, and in particular the second, *The Birth of Biopolitics*, is that they take for granted that liberalism and liberal techniques of government exist or have existed in opposition or as an alternative to the strategies of the state.

Indeed, liberalism—understood as a practice and theory situating itself between capital and the state in order to defend and augment the freedoms of the market and society—bears further scrutiny. Given neoliberal management of the relationship between the state and capital during the crisis, it seems to me more reasonable to test a working hypothesis of Deleuze and Guattari, who in *Anti-Oedipus* identify what gives capitalism "its appearance, the pure illusion, of liberalism." They come to a radical conclusion, one that proves decisive for interpreting the current crisis and its consequences: "[capitalism] has never been liberal; it has always been state capitalism."[1] In other words, the supposedly immanent functioning of production and the market has always depended on the intervention of sovereignty.

In light of the policies implemented since 2007, it is difficult if not impossible to dispute the interdependence of sovereignty and governmentality. Discussing Rousseau's conception of government in *Security, Territory, Population*, Foucault himself affirms that "the problem of sovereignty is not eliminated; on the contrary, it is made more acute than ever."[2] Yet the affirmation no doubt applies as much to the period preceding the crisis as, more broadly, to the entire history of capitalism.

Analysis of governmentality must focus not on the "suspicion that there is the risk of governing too much"[3] or on the "freedom" whose principles liberals allegedly produce and defend against the state, but rather on the alliance between the state and capital (between the "state" and "the market," as economists would say) and, therefore, on state capitalism. As the crisis has unequivocally shown, liberals, far from providing an alternative to state government, are only one of the possible forms of subjectivation of state capitalism.

There is never "any struggle against the very principle of state control,"[4] in other words, in capitalism there is no opposition between the principle of sovereignty and the techniques of governmentality, between the political and the economy. Interventions against monopolistic concentrations of power belong to a bygone era, when commercial and financial capital were still allied with the old system of production, and when nascent industrial capitalism [could] secure its production and its market only by obtaining the abolition of such privileges.[5]

Since then, rather than representing the freedom of society and the market against the state, liberals have contributed in a fundamental way to the construction of a sovereignty, a state, perfectly suited to capital.

But what state and what capitalism, what sovereignty and what governmentality, are we talking about? Is the state capitalism we see in the crisis the same as the state capitalism of the nineteenth and early-twentieth centuries? Can we still speak of state capitalism in Deleuze and Guattari's terms? Foucault's work can be useful as long as we interpret first ordoliberalism then neoliberalism as politics that seek a new configuration of state capitalism, a new relationship between sovereignty and governmentality, of which liberals constitute the subjective condition. Neoliberalism represents a new stage in the union of capital and the state, of sovereignty and the market, whose realization can be seen in the management of the current crisis.

That being said, the central thesis running throughout Foucault's lectures has been undermined more by the events that have shaken capitalism since 2007 than by any criticisms one might level against it. The crisis has largely undercut the notion that the problem of liberalism is "governing too much," that critique should focus on "the irrationality peculiar to excessive government,"[6] and that, as a consequence, "one must govern as little as possible." Neoliberal government centralizes and multiplies authoritarian government techniques, rivaling the policies of so-called totalitarian or "planning" states. That liberalism "consists in the maximum limitation of the forms and domains of government action"[7] is as untenable today as it is in retrospect.

How have liberals suddenly gone from wanting to govern as little as possible to wanting to govern everything? How is it that, whereas before 2007 they viewed all forms of "big government" as irrational, since then technocratic governments, Europe, the International Monetary Fund, the Central European Bank, all staunchly liberal institutions, have drawn up recovery "plans" for state budgets that cover the next ten or more years (the European Fiscal Compact calls for at least twenty years of "sacrifice" in order to pay back creditors)? How is it that they multiply institutions of control, supervised by "experts" who double-check the tiniest administrative spending; that they prescribe budget cuts down to the smallest detail; that they authoritatively set the time frames for balancing budgets; that they literally dictate laws to parliaments and national governments? How is it that the same liberals have replaced the "minimum state" advocated prior to the crisis with a "maximum state"? How does one explain this supranational neoliberal "big government" that, in the final analysis, has done just fine without "democracy"?

Obviously, there is something wrong with the opposition between the before and after, just as it is utterly reductive to think that the crisis has changed the nature of liberalism, that state intervention is conjunctural, and that once the crisis has passed, centralizing, authoritarian, intrusive government will become "liberal" once again. Today the state—and not in its minimalist iteration—intervenes in two ways instead of one. First, to save the banks, finance, and liberals themselves; second, to demand that populations pay the political and economic costs of the first intervention. Once for the markets, a second time against society.

But this is only one stage in a process that began with the birth of capitalism.

> Never before has a state lost so much of its power in order to enter with so much force into the service of the signs of economic power. And capitalism, despite what is said to the contrary, assumed this role very early, in fact from the start, from its gestation in forms still semifeudal and monarchic.[8]

The state and capital were indeed heterogeneous. The state is defined by a territory and borders. Capital has no territory; it is, rather, a process of permanent deterritorialization without any kind of territorial limit. The state constitutes a community, a people, a nation; capital is incapable of this, for competition, class divisions, and private appropriation ruins community, the people, and the nation. The state is founded on rights and citizenship, capital on the "interests" of entrepreneurs and the exploitation of workers, the population, and so on. The state exercises political sovereignty, bound to a territory and a population. Capital brings economic power to bear on a population whose only true dimension is the world market.

Governmentality (of which liberals, it must be repeated, are only one subjective form) first meant composing these heterogeneities then reconfiguring and subordinating state principles to the valuation processes of capital. One of the most significant turning points in the process of subordination came with the formation of the German social state, of which ordoliberals and, in a much more radical way, Carl Schmitt have offered the most lucid theorization. The introduction of the social state into the German constitution is, in addition to being historically important, relevant today as well, since the building process of European institutions and the euro originates in the ordoliberal techniques with which this new kind of state was constructed.

The economic state

Carl Schmitt, on the other hand, whose work has been used to promote the "autonomy of the political,"[9] has demonstrated that the social state marked the irreversible decline of the "sovereign" state such as Europe had known it. The social state no longer has political autonomy because it is occupied by the social and economic forces of capitalism.

The state is now entirely immersed in class struggle, in its conflicts and particular interests, which is why it can no longer represent the common interest, the "destiny" of a people, or the ethics of a nation. It can no longer be *super partes* because it has itself become the object of political-economic struggles and conflicts.

Neoliberals do not merely oppose the state in order to defend the freedom of society, they also work to mold the state, to transform it totally, so that it corresponds perfectly to capital and capitalist accumulation. *The Birth of Biopolitics* describes this new phase in the transformation of state capitalism by way of Foucault's analysis of the relationship between ordoliberals and the German state at the time of its postwar reconstruction. The defeat of Bismarck's Germany during the First

World War and of the Nazi state during the Second paved the way for what Schmitt calls a "new type" of state. "Given a state that does not exist, how can we get it to exist on the basis of this non-state space of economic freedom?" asks Foucault.[10] Through its "permanent genesis [...] from the economic institution," because "the economy creates public law."[11]

There is nothing spontaneous about the process. This kind of state must be constructed so as to be anchored in the functioning of the market; such is, according to ordoliberalism, governmentality's central task. Instead of the other of politics, the economy is the force that generates, directs, and legitimates politics. The market, instead of automatic and self-regulating, becomes the founding political bond, among other things, of state sovereignty.

> [T]he economy, economic development and economic growth, produces sovereignty; it produces political sovereignty through the institution and institutional game that, precisely, makes this economy work.[12]

As for the "economy," it must not be understood in an economistic sense by reducing it to a mechanism of production (the factory) or automatic exchange (the market). Foucault simply confirms Schmitt's analysis, published at the very moment the social state was formed: the sovereign state, the nation-state, the transcendent state, is dead and in its place rises the "economic state."

> In contemporary Germany we have what we can say is a radically economic state, taking the word "radically" in the strict sense, that is to say, its root is precisely economic.[13]

This is where a new conception of sovereignty takes shape, one in which the economy becomes indistinguishable from the state, political power from the power of capital, and governmentality from sovereignty. The latter no longer derives from the people, from democracy, or from the nation but from capital and its development, which entails a radical renovation of the concept of "state capitalism."

Governmentality does not "govern as little as possible"; its aim is to construct the "social state," an economic state underpinning the socialization of valorization whose target is society above all else. Germany and Japan did not enjoy an economic miracle because they no longer had to finance their armies (the military-industrial complex has never prevented economic valorization; on the contrary, it provides ample opportunities for the realization of surplus value), but more plausibly because, following their defeat, they constructed states completely "in keeping with the demands of the markets."

We speak of the German economy, but the economy is inseparable from the state; or better, in contemporary capitalism, we can no longer distinguish between the state, the economy, and society. Capital invests these three domains transversally while governmentality works to ensure their cohesion and harmony.

The neoliberal turn

The turn from ordoliberalism to American neoliberalism would deepen and intensify this new organization of state capitalism. The process of integrating and subordinating the state to economic logic would accelerate. The state would completely assume its new genesis in the market, to which it would abandon entire spheres of its former sovereignty.

On the one hand, governmentality drives to progressively weaken political and, in particular, monetary sovereignty in favor of the economy, submitting sovereignty to a process of privatization. Through taxation—another "regal" prerogative—the state acts on behalf of creditors and their supernational institutions. While these two state functions—regulating money and raising taxes—continue to be managed by the state, they are no longer the expression of its power as representative of the general interest, as guarantor of national unity; instead they represent the mechanisms of the supranational government of capital. On the other hand, governmentality must remain vigilant to ensure that the "economic state" maintains full and vigorous sovereignty over the population and society—a modality of capital's political control over class conflict and the "conduct" of the governed.

The subordination of administration and welfare to the valorization of capital which neoliberalism inaugurated in the 1980s is not indicative of a minimum state but rather of a state freed from the hold of wage-earners, the unemployed, women, and the poor over social spending. As the crisis has shown, the maximum state is altogether compatible with neoliberalism. The shift in the balance of power occurring in the 1970s enabled liberals to direct state functions (lender of last resort, fiscal policies, redistribution policies, etc.) to their own advantage.

The representative political system and the rule of law have met the same fate. Contrary to the claim Foucault seems to make (that the "participation of the governed in drawing up the law in a parliamentary system is the most effective system of governmental economy"[14]), the crisis has radically neutralized the voice of the governed, even in the case of elections.

Although its forms of expression have been profoundly weakened and utterly circumscribed by election laws, the media, and experts, the representative political system is still too democratic for the economy. Even reduced to the farce of the "participation of the governed," it still poses an obstacle to the governmentality of the crisis. The representative system is thus suspended, parties are divested of "power," parliament is reduced to registering the "orders" decreed by the institutions of world capitalism. Angela Merkel summed up the process when she spoke of a "democracy in conformity with the markets." Popular sovereignty is conditional, since the only vote that matters is that of the market and financial institutions of international governance, which express their "political" will every day and in real time via the stock market and the spread. If the people's vote agrees with these "grand electors," then the vote is legitimate; if not, the people will be asked to vote again or some other way of circumventing democracy will have to be found, one devoid of power.

Whatever democracy there once was in capitalism had nothing to do with liberalism or capital but arose out of class struggle and the resistance mounted by the "governed." On their own, liberals would never have ventured anything other than a democracy of property owners.

The social state as the government of society

This new iteration of state capitalism, the social state, was imposed according to the objectives of capital: the subordination of all social relations to valorization through the generalization of the logic of business. Ordoliberalism is the expression of a politics of the "market" whose priorities affect all of society. The subordination of society to capital would be fully realized first by way of financialization then through the economy of debt. Debt and finance constitute the apparatuses of evaluation, measurement, and capture of all social activity and not only that of labor. Ordoliberalism and neoliberalism represent two different modalities of capitalist government which are no longer limited to recovering industrial surplus but organize the appropriation of "social surplus value." Drawing on Foucault's analysis, we can follow the development of a governmentality now inseparable from the economic exploitation encompassing all aspects of social life.

From the end of the Second World War we begin the move from disciplinary societies to security (control) societies. The social dimension of production and the struggles of the 1960s revealed a subjectivity that disciplinary techniques could no longer control. Foucault sought to understand the articulations of a new power whose mechanisms no longer aim at a subject "confined" to a factory, prison, hospital, or school, but instead is exercised over "open" space, that of society. This new reality would lead Gilles Deleuze to recognize some forty years later that the problem of our societies is not confined man but indebted man.

Ordoliberalism inaugurated the process of constituting new techniques of governmentality. Ordoliberal governmentality must mold the state and the state must mold society in order for the market to exist, in order for the market to function as an "apparatus of capture" and measurement. If this double condition is not met—the "economic" state and the state of "economization of society" (Foucault)—the market cannot exist. The automatism and spontaneity of the market are produced and depend in large part on state intervention and its success, in other words, the conformity of society with capitalist accumulation.

For ordoliberalism, the market constitutes a "machine" that automatically finds the path to equilibrium. Yet unlike the market of classical liberalism, the market of ordoliberals is governed by competition rather than exchange. Instead of a mere natural game of appetites, instincts, and behaviors, competition must be produced, incited, supported, and protected. The governmentality of new state capitalism must intervene, as thoroughly as the Keynesian state, in order to arrange the *social conditions* of its existence. Competition and the market constitute a formal game that, like all formal structures, functions only under certain conditions which must be "carefully and artificially developed."

If "the main and constant concern of governmental intervention [...] must be the conditions of existence of the market,"[15] in order to guarantee its functions of measurement and appropriation, the state must act on data that are not directly economic in nature, that is, on the *social* sphere, on the population, techniques, education and training, the legal system, infrastructure, the socialization of healthcare consumption, culture, and so on. Governmentality must establish a "social policy" whose objective is to "take charge of social processes and take them into account in order to make room for a market mechanism within them."[16] The conditions that must be met in society are so numerous that it would be legitimate to ask if there really is something like an essence, a structure, that might be called the "market." It seems more accurate to say that the market is a political principle, a measurement, a model, forcing people, society, and the state (its system of administration and representation, etc.) to conform to the laws of the economy.

But what society do we mean? It is not a matter of establishing a market society, of normalizing and disciplining society, on the basis of exchange value but rather in conformity with the model of the corporation. The continuity between ordoliberalism and neoliberalism lies in the political project of transforming each individual into an "individual enterprise." Generalizing competition means

> generalizing the "enterprise" form within the social body or social fabric; it means taking this social fabric and arranging things so that it can be broken down, subdivided, and reduced, not according to the grain of individuals, but according to the grain of enterprises.[17]

Governmentality must socialize the "economic model of supply and demand and of investment-costs-profit so as to make it a model of social relations and of existence itself, a form of relationship of the individual to himself, time, those around him, the group, and the family."[18] Although realized by way of the corporation, the socialization of capital ("a policy of the economization of the entire social field, of an extension of the economy to the entire social field"[19]) has nothing to do with classical industrialization, for it is the entirety of social relations that must be managed like a business (managing the "individual home" like a business, "neighborhood communities" like a business, etc.).

To try to neutralize the conflicts of the "great factory," the nightmare of Fordist capitalism, ordoliberals dream of "an economy made up of enterprise-units, a society made up of enterprise-units,"[20] which neoliberals would attempt to establish starting in the 1980s, generalizing policies of "human capital" and promoting all forms of "autonomous labor." The "entrepreneur of the self," the model of neoliberal subjectivation, represents a kind of individualization of the corporation.

From this point of view, ordoliberals were somewhat ahead of Marxism, which was still confined to the factory and to the split between production and society. Only in the 1960s with the minor current of Italian Operaism would the relationship between capital and society be problematized. But few advances have been made since then, whereas capital has completely infiltrated society through the dominance of finance, debt, and these digital machines equipped with semiotic engines that we may describe as "constant *social* capital."

Neoliberalism would push corporate logic still further by making it an instrument for analyzing, measuring, and appropriating social relations, including the relation to the self or, indeed, between a mother and her baby. This is a politics of life (a "Vitalpolitik"). Already implemented by ordoliberals, it would be made more effective through finance than through the industrial corporation. The finance and politics of debt are, unlike the corporation, the immediately social apparatuses of government and capture that act transversally on the entirety of the population and society.

The great leap from ordoliberalism to neo-liberalism occurred in the transition from the hegemony of "industrial capital" to the hegemony of "finance capital"; state intervention in society is not challenged, however, but expanded. What changes is the nature of the intervention, some-thing the crisis has demonstrated. At the same time that it redefines the functions of the rule of law and rights, the debt crisis determines the kind of intervention these institutions can make in "society," and in a way that has little to do with liberalism.

Ordoliberals wanted "no economic interven-tionism, or a minimum of economic interventionism, and maximum legal interventionism."[21] The crisis has reversed the relationship between economic interventionism and legal interventionism or, to put it another way, legal intervention is directly, immediately, economic intervention. According to ordoliberal principles, the function of the market and competition has to be at once instituted, guaranteed, and regulated by a series of formal rules. Laws must define a general framework and never set a particular objective, never pursue a specific goal, such as promoting growth, full employment, a certain type of consumption, and so on. They must avoid imposing a choice the way an interventionist or "planning" state might and simply define the rules of the game such that the state is never in the position of "decision-maker." Instead, decisions devolve economic agents. Fixed formal rules must do no more than define an environment, a milieu, within which economic agents exercise their freedom; they must do no more than set "the rules for a game in which each remains master."[22]

It goes without saying that the relationship between the rule of law, the legal system, and "capital" has never worked this way. The crisis clarifies, as if there were any need, the nature of legislative intervention. Laws do not define "forms of general intervention excluding particular, individual, and exceptional measures."[23] On the contrary, laws are prescriptive; they not only determine a formal framework, set the "rules of the game," but prioritize certain contents—and in minute detail. They impose the flexibility required of the job market, define a tax system favorable to rents, cut pensions, social spending, etc. The "freedom" that remains to "agents" is the freedom to carry out orders. Laws and rules not only take society and the population as their object, they are also decreed against society, against the population. Despite what liberal ideology claims, intervention does not derive from the State of Law but from the institutions that "govern"[24] finance capitalism: private banks, the ECB, the IMF, and a handful of governments (like Germany's) that belong to the new regime of state capitalism.

Liberalism breaks with *raison d'état* in the name of society, Foucault tells us. It is "by reference to the latter that one will try to ascertain why government is necessary" and it is always in the name of society that liberals concern themselves with *raison d'état*: "How can one govern as much as possible at the least possible cost? Instead the question becomes: Why must one govern?" An entirely different logic is at work in the crisis. If the market does not function, if, instead of determining a "rational and fair price formation," it creates disequilibriums that block valorization and result in crisis, the fault lies with society itself. Although liberalism invented the narrative of a mythic struggle between the state and "civil society" driven by owners and entrepreneurs, nothing like this is possible now that society is composed of "debtors," now that governing must follow the interests of "creditors."

All evidence to the contrary, all logic, even the simplest "economic" logic, to the contrary, it is society that must change and conform to the markets, even if it means the disintegration of society, even if it means collapse, as in southern Europe. Hence the "counter-reforms" of the job market, cuts in social services, the fall in and freeze on wages, the rise in taxes on the poorest and middle class—all of it carried out with blatant cynicism in view of the "destruction of society" should society not cede to the extortion of debt. In order to align society and democracy with capitalist valorization, neoliberalism has given up on producing any kind of "freedom" as it zealously produces post-democratic authoritarian governmentality.

The euro, a German currency

Ordoliberalism constitutes the major political innovation on which the construction of European institutions is founded. The logic of European governmentality follows the ordoliberal model whose method of generating the "state" through the "economy" is applied nearly to the letter. This is why we can say that the euro is a German currency. The euro is the emblem of a new state capitalism in which it is impossible to separate the "economy" from "politics."

The media and experts harp on the absurdity of a single currency because political authority, a state (or a similar center of power), or a political community is apparently needed to legitimate and justify the currency. The euro has pursued and continues to pursue the opposite course, one grounded solely in the economy, hence its supposed weakness and inevitable failure. The view echoes nineteenth-century analyses of state capitalism; it fails to grasp the new bases and dynamics of state capitalism in the second half of the twentieth century, the capitalism invented and practiced by ordoliberals. The constitution is written by the economy, as Schmitt would say; and as the ordoliberals would say, the state is generated by the economy.

On the other hand, pro-Europeans would have us believe that the single currency represents an absolutely original advance over the nation-state. In reality, like sovereigntists, they miss what is at stake with the euro, namely, the construction of a new space of capitalist domination and exploitation. European governmentality seeks to construct a space and a population on a scale appropriate to the world market. The nation-state no longer constitutes a territory or a population capable of carrying out this project.

Contrary to what the sovereigntists claim, there is nothing absurd about the way in which the single currency was created; and contrary to what pro-Europeans argue, it does indeed represent an operation of power, a strategy commensurate with the new conditions of exploitation of state capitalism: a governmentality and capitalist sovereignty that seek, in order to establish themselves, a space other than the nation, a "community" other than national society. In this, European institutions follow the teachings of ordoliberalism: the state does not precede the economy (or the euro) but results from it. More specifically, the state is one of the articulations of this new apparatus of capitalist power which it has massively helped to create and maintain. The project does not aspire to the unity and cohesion of Europe, solidarity among its constituent populations, but a new apparatus of control and exploitation and, therefore, of class division.

The state and money

Obviously the process of building Europe presents more problems than that of the construction of the postwar German social state, which, despite its novelty, was confined to the territorial limits of a nation, a language, etc. The process of building Europe reveals intercapitalist conflicts that crystallize around different conceptions of sovereignty and, consequently, of the function of the state. Among European nations, France asserts the sovereignty of the nation-state in a paradigmatic way. Its position has long since been undermined by the German model of new state capitalism (and definitively so since the advent of neoliberalism). Yet it is still worth examining in light of French heterodox economics because the latter considers sovereignty in terms of money and debt, two "institutions" that get to the heart of the current crisis.

Money is the black hole of economic "science" in general but specifically of ordoliberalism. For the vast majority of economists money is exogenous to the economy; its functions (means of payment, measurement, general equivalent, etc.) serve merely to facilitate exchange. The picture Milton Friedman gives of this exteriority is emblematic: money is dropped on society from a helicopter, prior to which society produced without its help. Money comes into play only after production in order to exchange what has been produced. Money poses a problem for economists because its origin and functioning cannot be explained by the market (or by production) but rather by centers or sites of power established neither by exchange nor by competition or production.

Foucault, too, fails to problematize the most important "institution" of capitalism, that which expresses both in the most abstract and most concrete way capitalist relations of power. The limitations of his analysis correspond to the limitations of his reading of Marx. He stops at a description of the organization of labor in the factory, on which he bases, as he himself says, a large part of his theory of disciplines. But he overlooks the operations of capital as a process that through valorization traverses the three forms of capital ("commercial, industrial, and financial").

The transition ordoliberalism accomplishes from exchange to the corporation, from *homo economicus* as a man of exchange to *homo economicus* as an entrepreneur, which Foucault so expertly describes, requires us to consider money not only as general equivalent but also and especially money as capital, for the money of business is by definition money capital. The transition is fully realized in neoliberalism, where it is indeed money capital, that is, credit money, debt money, that organizes and controls the entire process of valorization.

The problematic advanced by Aglietta and Orléan's heterodox theory of money is quite original because, at its center, there is "a locus of power," the state and its monetary sovereignty, on the one hand, and debt, on the other. Although it offers a radical critique of the standard conception of money, the heterodox school not only firmly denies the existence of state capitalism, it makes the opposite argument, namely that "finance" (private money) and "central money" (state and/or public money) are today in direct conflict in their common claim to sovereignty.[25] The theory runs contrary to our hypothesis that in new state capitalism there is no conflict but rather convergence between finance, as the expression of the power of capital, as the *politics* of capital, and money, as the expression of the sovereign power of the state. The convergence occurs under the hegemony of finance capital (as collective capitalist), which in turn dictates its terms.

The heterodox school nonetheless marks an absolute difference with standard economic theory: money does not originate in market exchange but in debt. The innovation is immediately nullified by an interpretation of the functioning of debt based on a separation (or differentiation) of the economic from the political spheres, of society and the economy from the state. The state is said to function as a benevolent external entity which, by overseeing the actions of private actors, guarantees social ties. In capitalism there is supposed to be two forms of debt: economic debt and political (or social) debt. The first occurs in private contracts between individuals; the second results from the political logic of citizenship and solidarity and originates in the state.[26]

The social state and social debt are deduced from the autonomy of the political, which manifests itself through the mediation of class conflicts, because capital, with its divisions, "presents a permanent danger to national communities, a danger to which state action has had to respond."[27] The state, by virtue of its "exteriority," of its capacity to represent society in its totality, is said to have a pacific function aimed at the cohesion of the "living whole" (*le vivre ensemble*) of which social debt would be the political expression.

The idea that social rights follow from political rights is openly contradicted by neoliberalism and the transformations it has imposed on the welfare state. We still have citizenship, but we lose social services a little bit every day. If social debt depends on the state and on its principles of citizenship, why has welfare shrunk? It is the notion that social rights derive from political rights that is dubious. Here the judgment of the reactionary Carl Schmitt seems more relevant: social debt is the consequence of the class struggle for control of the social state and of its functions of appropriation and distribution.

What especially interests us in regulation theory is the function of the state. The state monetary institution, which operates at the junction of two financial networks—that of private debt and that of social debt—"works to produce the unity of society."[28] Debt is expressed in the same unit of account, sovereign money, within the same "national" monetary space, yet it does not carry the same values or the same force, because "politics" and its money, as a "public asset," take precedence over the economy and its money as a "private asset." Thus the dualism "remains within the control of a recognized sovereignty that subordinates monetary power to its authority." "Authority" should be understood as "a body of collective values for whose sake social cohesion is assured."[29] The function of the state as the "lender of last resort" is, once again, to safeguard social ties.

This theoretical description of the functioning of sovereign money does not at all seem to correspond to how it has behaved in the crisis. "Public" money has not operated at a distance from private and social debt; it has played an active part in the recognition and validation of debt. The state has recognized and validated private debt by paying it off (it has financed and continues to finance huge bank deficits) and it has neither recognized nor validated social debt, which it refuses to pay (it cuts and continues to cut public spending which the central bank refuses to finance). The lender of last resort only fulfills its role for private debt then passes the bill onto social debt (drops in spending and tax hikes). The state has not defended "society." On the contrary, through taxation and austerity, it has obliged society to pay for the "irrational rationality" of the market.

The preservation of social bonds has turned into its opposite, destroying society in certain cases (Greece) and, in others, radically weakening it (Spain, Portugal, Italy, France, the UK, etc.). Rather than stepping in to guarantee the continuity of social bonds, the political ("democracy") has been suspended in favor of complete "conformity with the markets" (Merkel).

By affirming as a constitutive principle of modernity the separation of economics and politics, of the economy and society, heterodox theory is unable to grasp the integral relationship capital has with the state and society. It completely neglects the process of progressive subordination both of the state and of society to the "market" by considering the process a mere "trend," the same trend that the crisis has made permanent. The hypothesis it rules out, that "the sovereign is capital valued by the market,"[30] seems to me the correct one. All the more so because in André Orléan's next sentence he perfectly describes what has occurred during the crisis: "This shift of power to the market reaches its ultimate phase when the power of valuation transforms into effective control." It is this "ultimate phase" that we are living through right here and now.

The contrast with Deleuze and Guattari's monetary theory is useful here for several reasons. For both theories, capitalism is characterized by a problematic, double monetary circuit (or by a double regime of debt). But Deleuze and Guattari propose radically different explanations and solutions, just as the capital-state relationship they deduce from them rely on different conceptions of capitalism.

Let us return to the terms of the problem such as heterodox theory defines it: the problematic duality arises between economic money[31] and sovereign money. The first is private money, "purely instrumental, which offers people solely its absolute neutrality, its impartiality." It is a "faithful instrument enabling the transactions of the market without disrupting it." Central state money, on the other hand, is a "public asset" and represents "society as a totality."[32] This is the money that assures the convertibility and validity of private money by establishing the cohesion of the whole, by guaranteeing the continuity of "living together." It is one of the multiple versions of the French "republican" perspective, although here it is expressed through money and debt—which is what interests us.

With Deleuze and Guattari, we leave the "Republic" to enter state capitalism. Without the distinction they make between money as a means of payment and money as capital and the subordination of the first to the second, it is impossible to understand the crisis. The heterogeneity of moneys does not have to do with public and private, individual and collective, but with the different functions of capital. The problematic duality arises between money as means of payment and money as capital, the first designating purchasing power and the second a power of control over labor and society.

For Deleuze and Guattari the two moneys do not have the same power. But whereas for heterodox theory the power differentials manifest themselves between economic money and state money, for the authors of *Anti-Oedipus* the power differentials concern "exchange money" and specifically capitalist money, money capital, credit money. State money guarantees the conversion between the two moneys and "dissimulates" class relations in monetary form.

On "anarchist" theory; or, how to talk about money while forgetting capital and capitalism

Before developing this point further, let us take a short detour that will allow us to underscore the different nature of the two moneys.

If anyone clearly establishes the distinction between credit money and commodity money, it is David Graeber in his book on debt.[33] And yet, based on the distinction, he constructs a kind of philosophy of history, one marked by cycles alternately dominated by credit money and commodity money. Since 1971 we have been in a cycle of credit money about which "nothing can yet be said," because forty years is nothing compared to the five hundred years these monetary cycles last on average.

This philosophy of history to which money holds the key surprisingly avoids confronting capitalism and its specific dynamic. Credit money and commodity money have a very long history; they were not born with capitalism, capitalism integrated them into its dynamic in a particular way. The emergence of "industrial capital" brought about a complete reconfiguration of the two moneys. They are no longer primarily in the service of centers of power—the king, the state, the bureaucracy—

but in the service of capital and its model of accumulation. Credit money is transformed into finance capital and commodity money into commercial capital. Along with industrial capital, they constitute the three forms of metamorphoses of capital and result in an economy that gradually and completely takes over society, nature, and the world. The process radically differs from how the two moneys functioned before the birth of capitalism.

The two moneys fulfill specific strategic functions in capitalist domination. Credit money represents the most deterritorialized form of capital; it is like a "flow of financing," which constitutes the true power and veritable "police" of capital. The "collective capitalist" is constructed from credit money. On the other hand, it is with commodity money that wages are paid and revenue distributed to the dominated.

Credit money as money capital embodies the logic of production for production's sake, in other words, the introduction of the infinite into capitalist valorization. The cycle of contemporary capital (M–M') begins with money and ends with money, which means that it never ends, that it must always begin again. The relationship between money and the "infinite" has always been with us, as has its power of deterritorialization, abstraction, and destruction of social relations. Until capitalism, societies strictly limited the relationship in an attempt to control it, erecting religious, political, and social systems precisely in order to avert its self-referential and infinite dynamic (money producing money).

Capitalism introduces something remarkably new because it constitutes and structures only one kind of society, that which turns money and its power of abstraction and deterritorialization into its organizing principle, its alpha and omega (M–M'), its meaning, and its purpose. Not only religious, political, symbolic, and social codes are, one by one, undone; all social and political relations must bend to its logic of production for production's sake, its logic of infinite valorization.

Capitalism marks a radical rupture in the history of credit money and commodity money, a rupture that eludes Graeber's categories. We have not entered a cycle in which credit money will now dominate commodity money for the next five hundred years, because with neoliberalism credit money, *as capital*, surpasses industrial and commercial capital. It is not a matter of one money dominating another but of the domination of capital (and its laws) over society—which is something else entirely.

Money, as commodity money and as money capital, expresses specific class relationships that did not exist in precapitalist societies. As means of payment, as "exchange money," on the one hand,

and as credit money, on the other, it constitutes and establishes class differences, that is, the power relations between capitalists and the dominated. Credit money expresses the "power" of capital whereas commodity money expresses the "power-lessness" of wage-earners. While Graeber clearly distinguishes the two types of money, he misses their different natures and functions *in capitalism* and, specifically, in the organization of contemporary power relations. Defining credit money solely on the basis of its virtuality, its "conventional" nature, is very reductive. One would do better to turn to the Marx of the *Grundrisse* for whom money as capital is a "claim to future labor," in other words, a right to exploitation and appropriation in the future. "Like the creditor of the state, every capitalist with his newly gained value possesses a claim on future labour, and, by means of the appropriation of ongoing labour has already at the same time appropriated future labour."[34] It needs only be added that the claims of contemporary capital do not appropriate labor alone but also other forms of social production.

Wage-earners and the population in general do not have access to money as a claim to current and future appropriation but only to the impotent monetary signs of the general equivalent, of money as means of payment, as commodity money, whereas capitalists have access to the signs of power of money capital, to the "flow of financing" that anticipates and determines future production. Wage-earners and the population can only exchange their money for commodities already available on the market, whereas capitalists and money as capital prescribe what is going to be produced, how it is going to be produced, the conditions for production, and the distribution of roles and functions. The conversion of the heterogeneity of the two moneys is guaranteed by private and central (state) banks.

Although private banks and central banks carry out different functions, they also operate in concert. Private money and public (or state) money work together and to the same end. Their actions have been absolutely complementary during the crisis, aimed at safeguarding the markets for which they are ready to sacrifice society, social cohesion, and democracy.

Orléan himself recognizes the subordination of "public" money to the logic of capitalist valorization. The power of monetary sovereignty is "contained within strict limits. It is difficult, if not to say impossible, for it not to validate private monetary creation."[35] The situation could not be otherwise, since private banks "hold the monetary initiative," that is, it is their money that functions as capital. Sovereignty (of the central banks) "plays only a subordinate role: faced with the legitimate credit needs of private actors, its mission is to manage the overall harmony of those needs."[36] One might doubt the legitimacy of the "credit needs of private actors," in particular those of banks, before, during, and after the crisis. Yet one must recognize the subordination of political and monetary sovereignty to a new center and apparatus of power. Indeed, instead of subordination, we should speak of the constitution of a new aspect of the apparatus of capitalist power, of which the state is a constituent part.

The new state capitalism

In order for us to understand the new arrangement of powers and techniques of governmentality, the crisis must not be interpreted according to heterodox theory as a conflict between politics and the economy, between public and private. The objective pursued is not that defended by zealots of the market like Hayek, who would like to eliminate sovereign money in order to replace it with a profusion of competitive private moneys. It is easy to see in the crisis that the capitalist apparatus has no reason to replace the state. The problem is rather how to integrate the state's "sovereign," administrative, and "regal" functions into a new governmentality whose administration it is not entirely responsible for.

Capital still needs the "sovereignty" of state money in order to assure the recognition and validation or non-recognition and non-validation of debts such as those currently overwhelming our societies. The purpose of this new, hydra-headed apparatus of power is not the "radical emancipation of the economic from the political"[37] in order to "isolate the economic sphere from all external, mainly political interference."[38] Heterodox theory interprets things upside down. Indeed, it follows the arguments of Karl Polanyi, for whom the economic order, formerly interwoven into the social fabric, acquires its "independence and distinguishes itself from society."

The crisis shows that there is no separation between the economy and society but rather complete subordination of society to the economy. Capitalism exceeds and integrates the dualisms of the economy and the social, of the private and the public, of the state and the market, and so on, by deploying a governmentality with multiple articulations. The power of capital is transversal to the economy, the political, and society. Governmentality is precisely a technique of assemblage, whose principal task is to articulate, on behalf of the market, the relationship between the economic, the political, and the social.

Neoliberal governmentality is no longer exclusively a "technology of the state," even if the state plays a very important role. Since the 1970s we have seen what might be called the privatization of governmentality. The latter is no longer handled solely by the state but rather by a body of non-state institutions ("independent" central banks, markets, rating agencies, pension funds, supranational institutions, etc.), of which state administrations, although not unimportant, are but one institution among others. This is exemplified in the actions taken by the Troika (IMF, Europe, ECB) during the crisis.

First, the state and its institutions promoted a rapid expansion in "privatizations." Likewise, they deregulated financial markets and encouraged the financialization of the economy and society. Then the same institutions applied the methods of private business management to the management of social services and the social state.

The crisis has thus made us real-time witnesses to the constitution and extension of a process Deleuze and Guattari call "state capitalism." The integration of the state and the market, of sovereignty and governmentality, of politics and the economy, of society and capital, has been pushed still further by exploiting the "shock" of the financial collapse. The liberal managers of the crisis have not hesitated to include a "maximum state" among the apparatuses of governmentality but a state that now exercises its sovereignty uniquely on the population. To free up the markets, liberal management imprisons society, intervening in heavy-handed, invasive, and authoritarian ways in the life of the population in an effort to govern all aspects of behavior. If, like every form of liberalism, it produces the "freedoms" of owners (of capital securities), it reserves for non-owners a mere semblance of what is already weak "political" and "social" democracy.

4

CRITIQUE OF GOVERNMENTALITY II:
CAPITAL AND THE CAPITALISM OF FLOWS

> *This is why we say in* Anti-Oedipus *that the essence of capitalism isn't industrial capitalism but commercial, bank, and monetary capital.*
> —Félix Guattari

In *The Birth of Biopolitics*, Foucault introduces a distinction between capital and capitalism which must hold our attention, for he presents at once a critique of Marxism and a new definition of capitalism. The two analyses and the link between them will allow us to grasp the partial convergences and the radical divergences between his understanding of capitalism, of liberalism, and of the relationship between sovereignty and governmentality and that of Deleuze and Guattari. The conception of capitalism developed in *Anti-Oedipus* asserts the impossibility or the illusory character of liberalism (the illusion of being able to separate government and sovereignty), whereas in Foucault liberalism is part of a sustained and original inquiry into different forms of government. The two volumes of *Capitalism and Schizophrenia* argue against separating finance and the real economy, considering them the two sides of a new *politics* of state capitalism and of a new function of sovereignty.

As everyone knows, Marx analyzes, dissects, and critiques "capital" but never uses the term "capitalism," which others would introduce later on. Foucault reproaches Marx and Marxists for identifying capitalism with "the economic logic of capital and its accumulation." It is impossible, he argues, to detach the economy from the institution. There is no single *capital*, "with its logic, its contradictions, and impasses"[1]; there exists only an industrial-economic, juridical-economic, capitalism such that "historical capitalism [...] is not deducible as the only possible and necessary figure of the logic of capital" and its accumulation.[2]

Capitalism is always "singular." There is an American capitalism, a German capitalism, a French capitalism, a Chinese capitalism, etc. They differ in the institutional forms of the capitalist mode of production. If this is true, then we can see how, within "a singular capitalism formed by an economic-institutional ensemble,"[3] it is possible to intervene by inventing new institutions and, thereby, to force capitalism to change. It is through the institution and institutional change that capitalism is restructured, modified, and comes to surpass crises that seem "catastrophic" and "definitive." Furthermore, the institutional and juridical are "not part of the superstructure," they are not in "a relation of pure and simple expression or instrumentality to the economy."[4] They are constitutive of capitalism. If the economy is an ensemble of "regulated activities," then there is no pure and simple economic reality: the "economic process and institutional framework call on each other, support each other, modify and shape each other in ceaseless reciprocity."[5]

The critique is in large part correct, although it concerns Marxists more than Marx. It certainly identifies a limitation of Marxism, which Guattari himself notes in an article from 1968.[6] Now, I am bringing in Guattari's considerations in this context for two reasons. First, because, although he makes the same critique of a revolutionary process whose principal handicap is attaching the "institution" to "capital," he retains the vital category of "capital," which, he deploys with Deleuze in order to ascertain the nature and dynamics of capitalism. Second, because unlike Foucault Guattari approaches the institution from the perspective of the dominated. For the dominated, the origin of the institution is revolution and not law or the state: "One could say that revolutions produce institutions," whose main preoccupation is group subjectivation.[7]

Revolutionary processes have failed because they have shown themselves incapable of integrating and thinking the institution. While the "institutions" born of the Soviet revolution (the "Soviets," among others) became mired in dogmatic repetition and rigid determinism, the New Deal and German ordoliberalism, by reconfiguring the institutional dynamic, profoundly changed capitalism. Capitalism is "largely ahead of the institutional creative capacity of socialist states" for which the institution remains a "subset" of production or "capital," as Foucault understands the term. And yet "it is impossible to separate the production of any consumer commodity from the institution that supports that production."[8] Socialist planning is unable to "establish an original form of social creativity," for it gives no autonomy or freedom "to the intermediary machinery," which is instead tightly controlled. The only institutions that seem to interest socialists are the state, the party, and the army.

We can therefore agree with Foucault that "capitalism" is not directly deducible from "capital" as Marx described it. Nonetheless, the current crisis suggests that we qualify the critique and perhaps reverse it. If capitalism is neither reducible to nor immediately deducible from capital, there is still a "logic of capital and its accumulation." Capitalisms are all different, but they are all affected, at various levels, by the occurrence of the same "contradictions and impasses" of capital, to use Foucault's terms. German *capitalism* is not the same as American capitalism because they are indeed made up of different institutions. But both have been shaken by the subprime crisis, in other words, by the crisis of a *finance capital* with its own logic as well as by specific contradictions and impasses, irreducible to institutional features, that affect institutions and, in particular, the state. Here we encounter both the impossibility of separating capital and capitalism and the necessity of distinguishing them conceptually and practically. Capital and the state, the economy and the institution, call on each another, but their relationship requires a reading fundamentally different from the one Foucault proposes.

Governmentality is a technique with a long history, but as capitalism has developed it has made biopower its own technique for the regulation, control, and production of subjectivity. According to our hypotheses, if capital requires both the state and governmentality, it must be rigorously defined and the ways in which the state and governmentality constitute its institutions must be apprehended. The state (or the institution) is the other, ineluctable face of the economy such that no separation, no autonomy, of the state, politics, or the institution is possible. The relationship between capital and the state, between capital and its institutions, can be apprehended rigorously through the concept of "inclusive disjunction," in which differences, however salient, necessarily combine.

The "concept" of capital

> *[They] are wrong in looking for the exclusive and fundamental origin of this rationality/irrationality of capitalist society in the contradictory logic of capital and its accumulation.*
> —Michel Foucault, *The Birth of Biopolitics*

Why is it important, contrary to what Foucault argues, to grasp the laws, the nature, and the contradictions of "capital"? Because the neoliberal turn essentially lies in the "liberation" of capital from its Fordist institutions and, once the latter are eliminated, in the transition from the hegemony of industrial capital (M–C–M') to that of finance capital (M–M'), which involves an entirely different institutional configuration.

The hegemony of "finance capital" over industrial capital is not a simple accident, the conjunctural outcome of financiers' greed. Rather, it is inherent in the very logic of capital and its accumulation.

The "liberation" of capital operated by neoliberalism was initially that of "money as capital." It marked a new and more intense phase of deterritorialization, beginning precisely and significantly with the declaration in 1971 of the inconvertibility of the dollar into gold. "Freeing" "capital" does not mean freeing its supposed self-regulatory power (the market), but rather its immanent movement of permanent disequilibrium, its systematic search for asymmetries and inequalities, the conditions of its valorization, in other words, of the appropriation and expropriation of social production that are its actual aims.

Capital, from which, according to Foucault, capitalism cannot be deduced, has been at the heart of the capitalist strategy to profoundly transform capitalisms. The latter are effectively, institutionally, different from one another, but starting in the 1970s all of them have promoted, pursued, and facilitated the liberation of capital through the construction of new institutions. Whatever neoliberals (and even Marxists) may believe, "capital" has its own logic and a specific mode of production, neither reducible to the market, competition, or the corporation.

Let us begin with Deleuze and Guattari's definition of capital. The first passage is taken from Deleuze's lectures on *Anti-Oedipus*, the second from the book itself.

[C]apitalism is fundamentally industrial, but it functions solely as commercial and bank capital, which sets the objectives of industrial production. And here this commercial and bank capital is no longer allied with precapitalist formations. It establishes its true alliance, that with industrial capital itself, an alliance that entails all kinds of violence, that is, all the pressure and all the power that bank capital has over the organization of production itself.[9]

In a certain way, Deleuze and Guattari argue, it is "the bank that controls the whole system" and it is financial flows that guarantee the subjective investment of desire.[10]

Their definition is practically Marxian although it already points to a hegemonic logic of finance capital that introduces a radical discontinuity in the history of capital and capitalism. Since the industrial revolution, the capital-labor relation has been at the center of valorization, relations of power, and politics. The concepts for apprehending this new phase are lacking. Yet the vocabulary of *Anti-Oedipus* (flows, decoded flows, codes, decoding, interruption of flow, connections and conjunctions of flows, surplus value of flux, knots, rhizome, etc.) proves particularly well-adapted to describing finance capital as an apparatus of capture and command. First of all, it introduces us to this new and more intense phase of decoding characterized by the destruction of the economic codes (full employment), social codes (the social state), and political codes (political parties) that governed social relations in Fordism.

Concentrating almost exclusively on "production," Marxism underestimated the economic and political hegemony that finance capital exercised over industrial and commercial capital as of the 1860s.[11] Finance capital unifies industrial and commercial capital into a coherent whole. It represents the purest and most general form of appropriation, one whose hegemony returned in the 1970s. The categories of *Anti-Oedipus* appear to me useful for accounting for another aspect insufficiently thematized by Marxism: the integration of the working class and of the population in general into capitalist valorization, first through mass consumption then through welfare. This integration is inseparable from the "culture industry," marketing, communications, cinema, radio, etc., in other words, from technologies of power that act on and through the production flows of subjectivity. These categories enable us to grasp the double deterritorialization of production and power apparatuses.

The process of deterritorialization essential to capital valorization did not occur all at once (Marxian primitive accumulation); it repeats itself with each new phase of capitalist domination and, far from applying only to labor, has gradually extended to all social relations.[12] It decreed a "general mobilization" through which different flows (of labor, services, communications, desire) were removed from the territory in which disciplinary capitalism had confined them (the factory, school, army, hospital, etc.). The capital-labor relation was delocalized (to a new territory), flexibilized (mobilized within the national territory); social-state services were indexed differentially to the mobility imposed on the labor force and on the population as well as privatized; the nation-state and its governmentality were undermined and eroded by the movement of capital, migration, and transfers of technologies, which, each in its own way, have no boundaries. The communication and information flows attached to the state were "unchained" and ceded to private capital, etc.

The strategic institution that supported and drove the greatest part of this general deterritorialization was money, which, freed from its weight in gold, became infinitely mobile and infinitely mobilizable. What was stable was put in movement, what was solid was made fluid, to a degree that would even have surprised Marx. Flows may move at different speeds, but they must all be subordinated and adapted to and be functional with the governing speed of money capital, the most liquid and flexible form of capital.

Money as capital

Why is financial and monetary capital, the force behind the neoliberal strategy of general mobilization, in no way a parasitic apparatus or a simple speculative system? Why can we understand nothing of contemporary capitalism if we oppose finance and the real economy? Because finance capital constitutes the form most appropriate to the concept of "capital." To speak like Hegel and Marx, it is capital's actualization. Instead of representing a degeneration of capitalism, financial flows fulfill its laws. The concept of capital becomes a reality not with industrial capital but with finance capital.

Finance and its accounting mechanisms are better expressions of the nature of capital than industrial capital because they are radically indifferent to the qualification of production (of automobiles, skills, yogurts, software, subjectivities, gender, etc.). Financial flows are also indifferent to the qualification of labor (industrial, cognitive, service, domestic, sexual, media, etc.); all that is relevant to them is drawing from these various forms of production and labor a surplus expressed in abstract quantities of money. This indifference asserts itself in a radical way because finance has no other end than the appropriation of monetary surplus regardless of the type of production and labor.

Finance operates at the junction of the time of current production and that of future production, at that of current and future appropriation. It not only processes current flows but also possible flows, flows of wealth to come, embodied again and forever in abstract quantities of money, money capital. These financial flows are also indifferent to the qualification of future production and labor, being responsive solely to the levels of future profitability.[13]

The "liquid" form of these securities reflects the essential mobility of capital, the speed of passing from one sector to another, from one country to another, from one profit rate to another. Mobility ("liquidity") fulfills the most rapidly and efficiently the fundamental "law" of capital. Constantly running up against its own limits (periodic depreciation of profit margins), capital must continually displace them, repeatedly reposition them a little further and on an ever-larger scale. Ceaselessly expanding its own limits, the liquidity of credit money is the best able to manage investments in new sectors, in new resources, in order to assure itself new profit margins. New investments and new appropriations in turn encounter depreciations in invested capital and must relocate again and again—ad infinitum.

The infinite in production

Capitalism is the first type of society based on the deterritorialization and decoding of flows that no longer depend on any kind of extra-economic code (production for the despot, for the state, for the community, for ritual consumption, etc.). In capitalism, there are no longer "values," there is only "value." Capital thus has no external limit aside from its own valorization, which means that—and this is something absolutely new—capitalism is also the first society to introduce the "infinite" into the economy and production. The infinite repetition of production, the infinite repetition of consumption, the infinite repetition of appropriation.

Despite the claims of neoclassical economic theory, the increase in production, consumption, or appropriation does not diminish their "marginal utility." In capitalism, Pareto's law, according to which the first glass of water you drink satisfies more than the last glass of water, no longer pertains. The law of capital states that the more you drink, the thirstier you are, the more you produce, the more you want to produce, the more you consume, the more you want to consume, the more you accumulate, the more you want to accumulate. Production, consumption, and appropriation provide no possible satisfaction. From a subjective point of view, the cycle of capital can be described as a series of desires/ frustrations that feed off each other forever. Drugs and addiction count among the ontological conditions of capitalism.

It is once again money that best captures this reality, because the cycle of valorization, beginning with money and ending with money, has no end. With money, the dynamics of capital contains within itself its own end, yet it is only with the cycle of finance capital (M–M') that the immanence of capital's functions coincides with its concept.

The infinite, by definition, can have no equilibrium. However economics would have it, capital does not seek equilibrium but rather its opposite, the continual disruption of forms of production and reproduction, sparing no sector of the economy and no part of society. Perpetual disequilibrium, permanently maintained asymmetry, constantly pursued inequalities—these are the actual laws of capital, exactly the contrary of what theories of general equilibrium claim.

The Marxian formula for finance capital (M–M'), in which the only economic reality represented is that of money, does not imply the end of industrial labor, of production and services, of media production, and so on. Nor does it imply the disappearance of forms of "outdated" exploitation like slavery. It simply states that finance capital processes flows, from the most archaic to the most modern or hypermodern, by translating them into abstract quantities of money, by capturing and appropriating them in this form.

Cynicism is not a feature specific to finance but rather to capital, whose purpose is not and has never been production, wealth, or "employment" —commonplaces worth remembering—but rather accumulation for the sake of accumulation.

The conjunction of flows

Yet capital does not develop simply by virtue of decoded, non-qualified, and abstract flows. It emerges only when these flows enter into conjunction with each other, in other words, when it arranges their exploitation (historically, the exploitation of labor flows). The becoming-concrete of the "real abstraction" (as Marx would say) constituted by deterritorialized flows occurs by way of the conjunction of capital flows and labor flows in industrial production but also, today, through the conjunction/exploitation of all types of flows (of services, sex, images, knowledge, "free time," etc.). The capitalist convergence/conjunction of flows no longer refers to consumption/consummation, as in primitive celebrations, or to the despot's privilege to consume. It is no longer tied to pleasure or the ritual destruction of surplus. It is production for its own sake, the material form of the infinite valorization of "money capital." It is as an abstract quantity that surplus becomes the exclusive goal of society.

In what way and through what apparatus is this conjunction assured? Always through money, although money as capital does not only solicit and incarnate the decodification and abstraction of all social relations. It is also and above all the expression of an asymmetry, a power relation, an economic relation of exploitation. More than the great *equalizer*, money represents the great *differentiator*. This is, moreover, the function that specifically defines money in capitalist society. Capitalism is a monetary economy in which the operations of money are not functional (facilitating exchange, measurement, accumulation, etc.) but political, because it expresses and sanctions power relations. If financial flows are indifferent to the various modalities of production and labor, they are, however, integrally "qualified" by asymmetrical relations of power.

By assuring the junction of flows, money expresses at once quantities and the heterogeneity of these quantities. The flows of purchasing power (wages and income) and the flows of money capital manifest this heterogeneity, for capital, on the one hand, and the flows of wages and revenues, on the other, have no access to, do not use, and do not deal with the same money.

A capitalist economy can function only by establishing the conjunction of flows (of labor, sex, the media, etc.) that convey exchange value, purchasing power, with flows of another kind. "Of another kind" means, strictly speaking, flows of another power, a higher power, expressed through money as capital, through money that no longer assures exchange value but a financing structure, in other words, the possibility of prescribing the new production and new allocation of roles and functions. In contemporary capitalism, the conjunction of flows and their exploitation are controlled by finance, that is, by the most deterritorialized flows, since it is finance that decides, by shifting capital from one country to the next, from one sector to another, where, how, and in what conditions to "produce." It is the standpoint of finance, the standpoint from which non-qualified flows are managed, that dominates the management of private enterprise, the management of public services, and the management of scholars and science, which, on the other hand, work to actualize this real abstraction.

Axiomatics and its axioms

Deleuze and Guattari define these operations of capital as an axiomatics that is no longer scientific but social in nature. Axiomatics is a social machine of control and capture. Rather than "production for the sake of production," what characterizes capitalism is "appropriation for the sake of appropriation," for which it is prepared to sacrifice everything, even "production." Governmentality and its apparatuses are strictly subordinate to it. The modalities of government ("govern as little as possible" or govern everything) do not depend on a logic or debate within liberalism but on the axiomatics of ownership. This is the principal lesson that we can draw from the current crisis.

Financial axiomatics is created, on the one hand, by the globalized economy and, on the other, by its models of actualization (and reterritorialization), which encompass not only the state, collective institutions (education, welfare, television, etc.), mass consumption, but also the neo-archaisms of religious fundamentalism, racism, chauvinism, sexism, paternalism, and so on.

Before examining all the implications of axiomatics, we shall simply describe how it functions. Axioms are "operative statements that constitute the semiological form of Capital and that enter as component parts into assemblages of production, circulation, and consumption."[14] By whom are they declared? How do they function? Is it a question of ideology? Why and how do they change from one phase of capitalist development to another?

In the debt crisis it is not hard to find answers to these questions. Axioms are declared by financial and banking institutions, the transnational political institutions that incorporate states as one of their component parts. They define the principles (to repay creditors, increase taxes, cut welfare services, streamline state budgets, etc.) from which economic policies and governmentality are derived; they constitute semiotic flows that enter into production in the same way as material flows; they change because axiomatics is, in fact, *a politics that confronts and adapts to changing situations.*

Defining the conjunction and regulation of flows through axiomatics and its actualization might seem quite abstract. And yet, axiomatics fits the reality better than other categories. The changes in capitalist phases, the periods of change from one model of accumulation to another, are moments when intense conflicts arise, the stakes of which are changes of axioms and of the models of their realization. *The Birth of Biopolitics* gives a very good description of how axiomatics functions and of its model of realization. Foucault concentrates on the enunciation and the implementation of the ordoliberal axioms governing the construction of the "social economy of the market." The debate in postwar Germany over the new constitution and social state was a political battle over axioms and, therefore, over the institutional configuration and modalities of "capital" subjectivation during that historical period.

In the transition from Fordism to financial capitalism we saw two struggles unfold: the first very intense, over the axioms of wages, welfare, and employment, between capital and its institutions, on the one hand, capital and the dominated, on the other; and a second, no less intense, among elites and within capitalist institutions themselves. Neoliberal elites had to fight for a long time against Keynesians in order to impose their own axioms.

One of the symbolic turning points from one phase to the other was a speech Margaret Thatcher gave to parliament during which she brandished a book by Friedrich Hayek, which signaled that a recomposition of power had taken place based on new axioms.

In axiomatics, language and statements do not indicate what must be believed but what must be done. This is a radical innovation with respect to Marx: semiotics are included in the infrastructure, surpassing the dualist analyses of structure and superstructure. Capital is a semiotic operator and sign flows enter into the valorization process of capital. Axioms constitute a component part of machines of production, consumption, and circulation. The economy is much more than economic.

The long development of liberal concepts and their progressive conjunction with the new capitalist subjectivity they helped to create were an essential part of the neoliberal machine. Compared to Fordism, neoliberalism was built on a more limited number of axioms (markets can self-regulate; lower taxes on the rich and on business are productive; unemployment is a choice; privatization is beneficial to everyone, etc.). Once the axioms were taken for first principles, the other variables were adapted to and aligned with them. When a profit margin of 15% is considered an axiom, employment, wages, labor law, and the location of production must necessarily adapt. The so-called laws of the economy are revealed to be political axioms. No one has ever demonstrated that lowering taxes improves economic growth, and yet it is a truism, an axiom, which, by establishing an independent variable, forces social spending and wages to function as mere adjustment variables.

During the debt crisis, the model of axiomatic actualization operates on still fewer axioms: reimburse creditors, drastically reduce wages and social services, and privatize the welfare state. Capitalist politics is hardly interested in complexity theories. On the contrary, it proceeds by way of successive simplifications, unilateral decision-making, and authoritarian decree. Faced with the urgency of the crisis, it has simplified to the extreme. The debt economy has basically been built on a small number of axioms while all complexity has been subordinated to, mobilized for, and directed toward their actualization. Capitalist politics uses extreme simplification not so much to control, by way of these axioms, the "demented" flows of money capital, the actual causes of the crisis, but to undermine and curb welfare flows, those depended upon and appropriated by women, workers, the unemployed, the poor, the young, and so forth.

Axioms subordinate flows to centers of control and decision-making such as the market, the state, banks, corporations, and different consumer industries. The axioms of debt fulfill this task vertically, in an authoritarian and centralizing way. This is why axioms have been reduced to a minimum.

The axiomatics of contemporary capitalism

Employing the concepts of axiomatics and axiomatic actualization, we shall describe how contemporary capitalism functions and the role that money as capital plays in it (monetary, fiscal, and financial policies).

Monetary and financial policies (money as capital) constitute apparatuses of conjunction/disjunction as well as of flow capture. They form an axiomatics because they treat the relationships between capital flows and labor, communications, services, sexual labor, etc., flows as functional relationships (of appropriation) whose nature remains unspecified. Functional relations are also and above all relations of power, for if money is indifferent to the content of production and labor, it is not indifferent to power relations. Financing flows establish and impose differences, asymmetries, and inequalities among "material" flows. Contemporary capitalism institutes new relations of power; its cartography is traced by the monetary, fiscal, and financial policies that make up actual "politics."

The point of view of "finance capitalists" (of the power block that manages money, including the state) is "axiomatic," in other words, completely different from that of capitalists involved in production, distribution, communications, and research, who only consider the functional relationships between flows, and this, only in terms of their "profitability." In reality, like all capitalists, the latter treat flows as abstract quantities expressed as money, organizing their conjunction in order to realize a profit. Unlike financial capitalists, however, they are directly confronted with the organization of labor and with the relations of power that make these flows possible in manufacturing, communications, and the service industry. The management of financial flows remains detached from the organization and relations of power of the corporation, services, and so on, although it both presupposes and informs them.

Financial and monetary axiomatics can only function if there are corporations, trade, a society, a labor market, welfare, a political and administrative system, military power, etc., that actualize it. Conversely, all these institutions receive from finance, money, and taxation the revenue and power they would be unable to obtain by themselves.

Financial capital is nothing without commercial and industrial capital; on the other hand, under the current conditions of capitalism, commercial capital and industrial capital exist only by virtue of financialization, since only this historical shift made it possible to eliminate the influence workers had exercised over industrial capital more or less effectively since the industrial revolution. Financialization enabled the intensification of globalization and involved the whole of society in the valorization process. By themselves, the instruments of industrial capital (even in its cognitive form) and commercial capital would not have been able to achieve this end.

Finance capital does more than capture value, it is one of the principal producers of value (as expressed in the formula M–M', money makes money). Nor does the financial sphere merely control and dictate the future economy or evaluate and measure the current economy. It constitutes and measures the value of an enormous mass of securities whose rise and fall in value are determined by a market with specific "laws" and functions. The market aims at appropriating time as "possibility"; on it one buys, sells, and assures possibilities. At the same time as it seeks to control possibility, it states what is impossible ("There is no alternative!"). Securities (of which "futures" is indeed a fitting term) are as real as the products of industry and the service sector, and "fictive capital," as Marx called it, has consequences on human beings that are not in the least fictive.

It is no longer accurate to speak of finance capital and industrial capital as separate realities, for the hegemony of a higher vector of abstraction like that of finance reconfigures all the flows of lesser speeds. These divisions are surpassed and integrated by a new capitalism that operates with new institutions, new forms of governance, a new political system, all adequate to this higher level deterritorialization. In order for capitalism to function, industry, services, the labor market, and all of society must be subordinated to the new norms of valorization, mobility, flexibility, and evaluation. The factory has been restructured as a corporation in order to turn it into a machine for capturing surplus value directly for shareholders (in France we have gone from 30% of profit distributed to shareholders in 2008, at the peak of the crisis, to 80% today[15]).

Financial axiomatics has multiplied the possibilities for appropriation relative to the axiomatics of industrial capital. The latter "only" governs and appropriates industrial labor, whereas the axiomatics of finance capital assures the government and appropriation of forms of industrial, pre-industrial, post-industrial, slave, traditional, social, and media production.

Finance capital goes beyond appropriating flows, it configures them for the sake of its own valorization. The accounting standards imposed by finance on business and public spending (welfare) have precisely that purpose: translating this or that codified relation attached to a production or service into a measurable "flow" in accordance with the principles of financial valorization. But the true accounting reform is that of "tax havens," shadow banking, and all the fiscal procedures that permit corporations and the rich their global racket of legally not paying taxes.

The digitalization of society powerfully contributes to the operations of mobilizing and fluidifying everything that was once stable and fixed. It does so by joining the mobility of flows of production, communications, and services with the mobility of capital thanks to digital machines and the semiotics that make them function. There is therefore no opposition or contradiction between finance and the real economy because the latter has been completely broken down and reconfigured by the former.

Now that we have clarified the relationship between finance and the real economy, let us return to axiomatics. Axiomatics allows us to answer the questions raised by the deterritorialization (abstraction) of social relations. All societies once solved the problem of decodification that money introduced by establishing extra-economic codes (whether religious, social, or political). When money is the only "code" compatible with capital, how can flows be controlled, how can their conjunction and appropriation be regulated? Who assures the conjunction, exploitation, and appropriation of flows when extra-economic codes no longer function?

In an infinite process, codes are useless because they interrupt processes by virtue of their specificity, their particularity, by the fact that codes are, precisely, extra-economic. Once there is no longer any extra-economic code to limit and orient production and once the dynamics of production are "confined" to the infinite, all that remains is an apparatus that deals exclusively with the functional relations (profitability) between its abstract and non-qualified elements.

This is something utterly new in human history: capital substitutes extra-economic codifications for an axiomatics of abstract quantities and their relations. Money as capital deploys this logic in an exemplary way not only because it establishes functional relations (of power), but also because, like scientific axiomatics, it directs, processes, and controls the infinite (M–M'). "Axiomatics is a finite network applied to infinite material"[16] in order to master, regulate, and control the schizophrenic movement of capital. It constitutes "a stopping point, a reordering that prevents decoded semiotic flows [...] from escaping in all directions" and, in so doing, permits appropriation.[17] Axiomatics defines the framework in which governmentality operates.

The state as model of realization

Thus the states, in capitalism, are not canceled out but change form and take on a new meaning: models of realization for a worldwide axiomatic that exceeds them.
—Deleuze and Guattari, *A Thousand Plateaus*

To go from "capital" to "capitalism" as Foucault understands the term, that is, as inseparable from the institution, we must move from axiomatics to its model of realization. After having extended and enriched the Marxian definition of capital through the apparatus of conjunction and exploitation of non-qualified flows, Deleuze and Guattari add that "This [...] is only one very partial aspect of capital."[18]

The axiomatics of capital, which deals only with abstract decoded flows, assuring only functions and relations between non-qualified flows, recognizes neither man nor woman, neither sex nor gender, nor body, ethnicity, race, or nationality. In these flows of deterritorialized money, there are no subjects, objects, individuals, collectives, professions, or trades. On the other hand, in order to be realized concretely, axiomatics must necessarily produce and reproduce the same "qualifications" that money, the great equalizer, erases, by establishing not only class but also racial, gender, and social divisions and hierarchies.

The passage, conjunction, and dynamics of decoded flows, driven by the infinite and proceeding through ruptures and upheavals, demand regulation and governmentality. Until the 1970s, the state served as the principal model of realization of axiomatics, limiting the higher speed of capital deterritorialization[19] and providing it with "compensatory reterritorializations," of which the "nation" was undoubtedly the most important. From these "compensatory territorializations" were built the institutions, values, and subjectivations that eluded capital—capital as the abstract machine processing decoded flows. The nation-state here becomes the model of realization of the axiomatics of capital insofar as it assures "the passional and living forms in which qualitative homogeneity and the quantitative completion of abstract capital are first realized."[20]

From the beginning and on a global scale the capitalist machine has worked to destroy the old forms of production of subjectivities (traditional, corporate, tribal, communal, etc.) in order to make them "available" for exploitation. The flows of subjectivities "freed" from prior social codifications must be "formatted" by state institutions (school, army, hospital, healthcare, etc.), which assign to individual subjects a body, a gender, a race, a nationality, and a subjectivity that function within the social division of labor. Foucault brilliantly describes the functioning of institutions that forge and normalize sexuality, subjectivity, and the body. But what interests us is financial axiomatics as a framework both promoting and limiting these institutions, because it can demand not only their transformation but also their destruction. The closing of schools, universities, hospitals, administrations, and cultural institutions imposed on Greece does not represent a limit case but rather a laboratory for neoliberal governmentality. Turning apparatuses of governmentality to authoritarian ends, suspending or nullifying them in order to install in their place non-democratic forms of government—this is the grand experiment of the crisis.

The capitalist machine requires "personifications"; as in Marx, the capitalist and the worker are personifications of industrial capital relations. The sexualization, racialization, and nationalization of subjectivities, dimensions unknown to axiomatics, are products of the state model of realization and the conditions for the formation of the labor force and the population.

The New Deal and the social-democratic policies[21] of the postwar represent the most advanced form of the realization of axiomatics by the state.

The Fordist model of axiomatic realization adds to the institutions, laws, "compensatory territories," and forms of subjectivation/subjection proper to the "nation-state" those of the "social" state. The abstract and decoded flows of capital are reterritorialized not only by way of the "political" system (the citizen, the legal subject) but above all, beginning with the New Deal, through the solidarity of the welfare-state social system. The personification of the "user" of social services indexed to employment go along with and complement another personification, unknown to nineteenth-century capitalism, that of the "consumer."

State intervention is all the more intense and widespread because the "realization of axiomatics" must respond to, integrate, and neutralize the revolutionary upheavals that traversed the twentieth century as well as "regulate" the destructive power of late-nineteenth and early-twentieth century liberalism that led to the greatest massacre in human history. Fordist axiomatics and its realization conclude a period of civil wars the European bourgeoisie had unleashed against the working class and the October Revolution. It is the "realization"/integration once carried out by that state that has so thoroughly failed neoliberalism today. Neoliberalism has thus been forced to deterritorialize both Fordist axiomatics and its model of realization (the nation-state).

One by one, worker struggles and social struggles, women's and students' struggles, eroded the "compensatory territories" and institutions that realized the axiomatics. Under the pressure of these struggles, capitalism was obliged to rid itself of the state and social sphere that posed obstacles to its valorization (depreciation of capital). Post-Fordist axiomatics thus no longer provides a suitable mode of subjectivation and subjection, for financial capitalism weakens political and social representation, on the one hand, and, on the other, weakens the legal subjects, political subjects, and social subjects of Fordism by replacing them with the entrepreneur of the self, human capital, the hyperconsumer, in short, by figures driven by the competition of all against all, the intensified individualism and social Darwinism in which each person can only count on himself. The realization of axiomatics functions on the same principles as axiomatics itself, reinforcing the "schizophrenic" deterritorializing tendencies of capital instead of attenuating or regulating them.

The relationship between axiomatics and its realization is also at work in the debt crisis. The management of real-estate loans and their transformation into securities tradable on financial markets have been carried out exclusively in terms of monetary and financial flows and of their functional relations in view of continually expanding credit, without taking into account the real situation of debtors (access to income, poverty, etc.), in other words, without taking into account their model of realization. This behavior, which considers only the functional relations between flows and their profitability, and which pushes both as far as possible, does not represent incompetence on the part of "economic agents," nor any particular "greed" on the part of traders, but rather a "law" of capitalism ("capitalism would send its flows to the moon if it could"). Once the crisis exploded, state intervention was imperative not only to save the banking system but also to transform the conditions of realization.

The crisis first imposed a change of axiomatics and its realization. From an axiomatics of credit we moved to an axiomatics of debt, which transformed those who had obtained credit into insolvent and culpable debtors. Then, after a short period of hesitation, the debt crisis was used to restructure the conditions for realizing axiomatics, that is, to sweep aside all that still resisted financial reorganization (the residual power of wage-earners and the residual power of social actors over welfare) and to accelerate privatizations—the other face of the debtor-creditor relation.

All the impasses to the realization of neoliberal axiomatics have crystallized in the crisis; the integrating force guaranteed by the social state and state of law no longer exists. The realization of the axiomatics of debt produces a personification of the capitalist relation in the negative and regressive figure of the indebted man, to whom a state progressively freed from its social burden and from democracy has little to offer besides austerity, the imposition of new sacrifices, recession, and budget cuts. The axiomatics of contemporary capital thus calls for an authoritarian model of realization.

Axiomatics is neither an automatic nor a transcendent machine

While capitalism thus proceeds by means of an axiomatic and not by means of a code, one must not think that it replaces the socius, the social machine, with an aggregate of technical machines
—Deleuze and Guattari, *Anti-Oedipus*

Better than other apparatuses axiomatics helps us to understand the functioning of capitalism and the forms of its governmentality because it allows us to avoid two errors: it prevents us from reducing them, first, to a mere subjective power and, second, to an impersonal and automatic power exercised by technical or cybernetic machines.

Capitalism would have us believe that it functions like an automaton, that there is no alternative precisely because the market, the stock market, and the debt economy are governed by automatic operations (and their cybernetic, self-regulating feedback), and that the forms of governmentality function in the same way, such that populations can do no more than adapt, reduced to the role of adjustment variables. Stock market prices rise and fall and it is up to the population to respond to these signals by adapting its behavior in real time to the variations, just as a thermostat reacts to variations in temperature.

Capital considers that the social machine functions no different from a repetitive, self-regulated, depoliticizing automaton. In reality, when automatic mechanisms function, it is always the result of a political victory over conducts. Automatisms represent the normalization of conducts, the specific effect of which is to depoliticize political action. The automation of the market, when it occurs (or seems to occur), never results from the simple operations of a technical machine, be it cybernetic, but from a social machine. Axiomatics (and its model of realization) has nothing technical about it; it is a political apparatus. It proceeds through experimentation, trial and error, advances, setbacks, and, therefore, through a politics that "implies social organs of decision, administration, reaction, inscription; a technocracy and a bureaucracy that cannot be reduced to the operation of technical machines."[22]

The social machine of axiomatics is neither an automaton nor a cybernetic machine capable of self-regulation[23] because it must follow the variations in the movements of capital and relations of power that never tend to equilibrium. Neither operates through equilibrating feedback but rather through ruptures, destruction, upheavals, and crises.

In the financial crisis, machines (90% of stock-market trades are done automatically) in no way guarantee self-regulation. On the contrary, their automation often amplifies disequilibriums. Machines do not demonstrate autonomy because they always function within assemblages of power of which they are mere component parts, open and connected to alterities and exteriorities, the most important of which is once again the dynamics of "capital" and its valorization. The latter command the machines. For "it isn't machines that make capitalism, it is capitalism that makes machines" (Deleuze and Guattari) by integrating them into its operations. The "success" of globalization ensured by the market and intelligent automata has led to systemic crisis because there can be no self-regulation or self-government through technological mediation.

Axiomatics, the social machine that integrates both the "systemic" necessities of capital and the political imperatives of social control, is capable of effectuating very rapid change. Within what Foucault calls security societies, in which power might consent to "a whole series of different, varied, and even deviant behaviors,"[24] and in which its exercise will consequently be "more skillful, more subtle," tolerant of a certain "pluralism," we witnessed in the first phase of neoliberalism the economic exploitation of the production of "differences." In the current phase, which succeeds that of the "Belle Époque," we have seen an authoritarian turn in governmentality in which power is exercised without much "subtlety" and only the "pluralism" of financial flows is tolerated. The distinction between disciplinary and security societies is quite useful as long as we remember that both are above all societies of capital and that governmentality changes depending on whether control over the economic cycle is exercised by industrial capital or finance capital.

The governmentality of debt

There is not a succession of law, then discipline, then security, [...] security is a way of making the old armatures of law and discipline function in addition to the specific mechanisms of security.
—Michel Foucault, *Security, Territory, Population*

In a remarkable reading of Foucault, Frédéric Gros observes that governing does not mean "to submit, to command, to direct, to order, to normalize," since it is not a matter of an apparatus expressing the power of one will over other wills. Confronted with events that possess their own specific dynamic, confronted with "realities" which Foucault defines as "natural," such as flows of production and flows of finance, which, as such, are not human (with which one cannot establish an intersubjective relation), governmentality "imposes nothing. No physical force, no prohibitions, no norms of behavior."[25] Through a "series of flexible, adaptive rules," it incites the creation of a milieu that compels the individual to react in one way rather than another.[26]

Here again the categories Foucault introduced at the start of neoliberalism must be put to the test of the current crisis. Governmentality does more than incite, solicit, and facilitate; it prohibits, standardizes, directs, commands, orders, and normalizes.

All the functions that security "regulations" are supposed to exclude are therefore adopted, managed, and imposed in the political phase that began with the 2007 crisis. The realization of axiomatics is accomplished, as Foucault himself says, by accumulating different forms of power—sovereign, disciplinary, security power—and not by substituting certain ones for others. The crisis prioritizes the sovereign and disciplinary exercise of power within a security society by establishing authoritarian governmentality.

In the crisis, governmentality clearly corresponds to a way of exercising power that Foucault abandoned once he moved from the analysis of disciplinary societies to that of security societies.

> The daily exercise of power must be considered a civil war: to exercise power is, in a certain way, to wage civil war and all the instruments, the tactics, one can identify, the alliances, must be made analyzable in terms of civil war.[27]

Is the claim that power "is not what suppresses civil war but what wages and prolongs it" only valid for disciplinary societies?

Power does not come after civil war, it does not succeed conflict as pacification; nor is civil war what comes after power, when power would finally disappear in the confrontation of all against all.

Division, conflict, and civil war structure power and the political by constituting a "matrix within which elements of power come into play, are reactivated, dissociated."[28] Foucault's arguments are obviously no less relevant to the situation today. Governmentality is the mode of control of this dynamic in security societies.

The problem with Foucault's liberalism—"to govern as little as possible"—is directly linked to the possibility of multiplying the apparatuses of governmentality (of the conduct of conducts), to their diffusion and capillary distribution, to their horizontal and "environmental" operations. But when, as is the case in the present crisis, these apparatuses undergo a sovereign centralization and a partial (Spain, Italy, Portugal, etc.) or radical (Greece) destruction, a "kind of homeostasis," a "global equilibrium," or "actuarial" or "regulatory" equilibrium, is not what we see. What we see is "civil war" as a possibility, as a strategy, as a mode of "government" of the population. The possibility of destruction, effectively realized, directly concerns and affects the concept of governmentality.

Civil wars, battles, conflicts, and the "history of the displacement of wealth, of exactions, theft, sleight of hand, embezzlement, impoverishment, and ruin"[29] are what make "governmentality" intelligible. It is urgent that we return to the Foucault prior to his theory of governmentality and to his program of "struggle against economic knowledge," for the debt economy demands that we dig "beneath the problem of the production of wealth so as to demonstrate that it was ruination, debt, and abusive accumulations that created a certain state of wealth."[30] An economic theory of value is therefore less necessary than the political question: "who won and who lost, [...] who became strong and who became weak" in neoliberalism? "Why did the strong become weak, and why did the weak become strong?"[31] Knowledge is always partisan knowledge that must be constructed through conflict and struggle rather than deduced from the economy.

"Destruction" (impoverishment, ruin, debt, etc.) is one form of the exercise of power that one finds both in sovereignty and in disciplines and control societies. At certain times and under certain conditions, it becomes the core of capitalist strategy. Of course, power is always distributed; it is never the object of exclusive possession; power is not concentrated above, it comes from below; power is not monolithic but can become monolithic in certain circumstances and for a certain length of time. Foucault's theory of the exercise of power remains fundamental, but it must each time be related to the situation, to the actual power plays in capitalism, and must not exclude civil war or class struggle. After the crisis of 1929, capitalism multiplied the apparatuses and techniques of "governmentality" in order to prevent relations of power in the political sphere from turning into open conflict.

The "conduct of conducts" is better able to exercise control in a financialized, highly socialized, uncertain and unpredictable economy because it is entirely oriented toward the future. And yet capitalists, and especially financial capitalists, although they solicit, incite, and facilitate governmentality, know very well that the matrix of power relations is division, antagonism, confrontation, that its logic is that of the victor and the vanquished, that it is a question of what the richest and most famous of American financiers calls "class warfare," even if most of the apparatuses are not explicitly warlike. The intensification of the crisis has unified a political class that modifies the techniques of power according to the absolute priority of safeguarding property.

Actuarial techniques against the accidents of life (unemployment, illness, old age, etc.) are more than mechanisms of a security power more "subtle" and less "vulgar" than disciplines, for they are violently subordinated to and made to function with a new form of class struggle. The concept of biopolitics must be somewhat qualified, since the power to "make live and let die" is subject to the logic of property embodied in the new neoliberal social model. If you can pay, you can live, and if you cannot pay, you can die, insofar as your exposure to death, to the risks of social death (impoverishment, misery, exploitation, domination, inequalities) and political death (exclusion, rejection), increase. Biopower and governmentality are subject to the axiomatics of capital.

Capitalism is not only "repression," it is also and above all "production," although of a specific type—production always coupled with "destruction." The destruction of humanity by nuclear technology (military or civil) is one possibility that looms over society just as ecological catastrophe threatens the planet. In each capitalist phase the displacement of the limits to valorization and appropriation resembles a "bad infinity," because capital runs up against impossibilities which it can overcome only by turning Schumpeterian "creative destruction" into destruction *tout court*. Deleuze and Guattari's anti-production becomes radicalized in certain phases of capital's cycle by destroying machines and human beings (constant capital and variable capital). This is the other, complementary side of liberalism that followed the "Belle Époque" (that of the early twentieth century as well as of the 1980s and 90s).

In conclusion, we can return to our point of departure. We began by asserting the impossibility and illusory nature of liberalism. Just as there has never been liberalism, capital has never had a progressive or modernizing side. As Guattari reminds us, the process of capitalist deterritorialization, which involves "the continuous disruption of production, the ceaseless dismantling of social categories, insecurity and eternal movement [...] all the while referring to universalizing perspectives, has, historically, never been able to achieve anything but withdrawal into itself, nationalist, classist, corporatist, racist, or paternalist reterritorializations."[32] Capital is thus driven by a dual movement. What it "liberates" from the religious, social, and political codifications that preceded it, it immediately subordinates to another apparatus of power. The two movements are simultaneous and inseparable.

> The history of capitalism [...] entails a generalized decoding of flows and at the same time something more, as if capitalism had to establish an apparatus dedicated to conjugating decoded flows. That is what gives capitalism its appearance, its pure illusion, of liberalism. It has never been liberal; it has always been state capitalism.[33]

Contemporary sociology commits the same error when it defines contemporary society as "liquid." Capitalism does not "liquefy" social relations, the economy, or semiotics without at the same time solidifying them, without at the same time petrifying class differences, solidifying as never before private property and patrimony, petrifying social mobility, solidifying and intensifying exploitation, and so on.

In a certain way, capitalism is madness in its purest form, since deterritorialized flows of money ruin every code (just as the insane ruin the codes of social signification). But it is also the absolute opposite of madness, for flows are blocked and absorbed into an axiomatics, into an accounting system which, instead of allowing flows to pass through, arrests and subordinates them to machines of power, control, and decision. When property has been threatened in the crisis, capital has had no difficulty subordinating flows to axiomatics and, if necessary, destroying them altogether.

This is where we meet up with Foucault's capitalism, although in a completely different way, with completely different functions. Capitalism is indeed the other face of capital, but without capital and its "destructive" side, the forms of governmentality of the economy, of society, and of behavior would remain incomprehensible.

5

CRITIQUE OF GOVERNMENTALITY III:
WHO GOVERNS WHOM, WHAT, AND HOW?

Maybe speech and communication have been corrupted.
They're thoroughly permeated by money—and not by
accident but by their very nature. We've got to hijack
speech. Creating has always been something different
from communicating. The key thing may be to create
vacuoles of noncommunication, circuit breakers, so we can
elude control.
—Gilles Deleuze, *Negotiations*

Having reconstructed a concept of capitalism in
which capital and institutions constitute the two
sides of the same coin, we shall attempt to develop
Foucault's pioneering work on governmentality
and identify how it has operated during the debt
crisis. For Foucault, governmentality is fundamentally a state technology whose purpose is to govern
people and their conduct. In response to numerous

criticisms, claiming that his theory of power failed to include a theory of the state, he argued that governmentality was to the state "what techniques of segregation were to psychiatry, what techniques of discipline were to the penal system, and what biopolitics was to the medical institutions."[1]

Based on our concept of capitalism, we can ask with renewed relevance: Who governs whom, what, and how in contemporary capitalism and in particular within the debt economy? The state? Finance? Private enterprise? And what exactly does one govern in capitalism? Only people's behavior (or conducts)? And with what techniques? Those the state has put in place? To give a synthetic response developed below, we can posit the following: In contemporary capitalism, one governs social machines (axiomatics) and subjectivities for these machines (the realization of axiomatics). The constitution of "political economy" is inseparable from a "genealogy of morals" that produces and governs the formation of a labor force in the broad sense of the term, for the latter today includes a subjectivity for consumption, for communications, and for services. Deleuze and Guattari never spelled out a theory of governmentality, and yet, with their understanding of the operations of capital, they gave us the categories necessary for thinking the nature of governmentality and regulation in contemporary capitalism.

Starting in the 1920s, governmentality appears as an ensemble of techniques that cannot exclusively be attributed to the state. Private enterprise would become hugely invested, through consumption, marketing, advertising, cinema, communications, and so on,[2] in the government not only of individuals and their behavior, but also of preindividual elements, modalities of perception, ways of feeling, seeing, and thinking. Private enterprise does more than simply manufacture merchandise; it produces worlds and endows them with values, lifestyles, an unconscious—"incorporeal" instruments of governance as efficient as the most corporeal techniques.

Even with regard to "governance," capitalism is "state capitalism," since "private" capital, with its techniques of production of subjectivity and valorization, takes upon itself the creation and control of individuals as well as the preindividual and incorporeal elements that they constitute. The state, of course, through welfare, social services, collectives, and so on, continues to play an important role in the production of subjectivity, but its governance is henceforth "privatized"; business management becomes *the* method of administration. State property continues to be "public" but it is now devoted to the profitability of "private" property. Public and private converge in two ways, because together they constitute an apparatus for the valorization, production, and governmentality of subjectivity, of a genealogy of morals. Capitalist valorization and the production of subjectivities coincide.

Machinisms

One of the limits of contemporary critical thought, with the remarkable exception of Deleuze, Guattari, and Simondon, lies in the almost total absence of a concept of the "machine," even though capitalism is above all a machinism and even though today the production of subjectivity and the techniques of governmentality are inconceivable without the intervention of machines. Critical theories seem to have forgotten Marx's lesson on the essentially machinic nature of capitalism:

> *Machinery* appears, then, as the most adequate form of *fixed capital*, and fixed capital, in so far as capital's relations with itself are concerned, appears as *the most adequate form of capital* as such.[3]

The organization of capital (and, consequently, its techniques of governance) is not centered on individuals or on the social sphere. Individuals and their behavior are not a starting point but rather the result, an endpoint. Capital is a social relation, but this "relation" must not be reduced to inter-subjectivity and/or interindividuality. It encompasses more than human beings and their behavior, for the latter are only component parts of capitalism. Capital is indeed a relation, but a machinic one, insofar as it does not exclusively involve "subjects," subjects whose activities would constitute a spectral objectivity in turn dominating them, as is the case in Marx.[4] It also involves a growing number of non-humans. Relations of power are already and immediately exercised by social and technical "machines."

Within the organizational forms specific to capitalism (manufacturing, communications, finance, etc.), man and machine are not opposed as subject and object. Subjectivity—now that modernity has completely emptied the world and nature of all "spirits"—is not situated exclusively in the human subject (or, for Marx and Marxists, in "living labor").

Deleuze and Guattari refuse to attribute to human subjectivity an "exceptional existential status" and argue that forces other than consciousness and language can function as "vectors of subjectivation" or as "sites of enunciation." This includes machines, even if they do not speak. To say that machines (and signs, objects, diagrams, etc.) constitute sites of proto-enunciation and proto-subjectivation means that they *suggest, enable, solicit, incite, encourage, and prevent certain actions, thoughts, affects, and promote others*. Very significantly, Foucault uses the same verbs to describe how power relations function: machines and signs, he says, act as "an action upon an action," which must not only be understood as a relation of one human being with another. Just like humans, non-humans play a part in defining the framework and the conditions of action. One always acts within an assemblage, a collective, in which machines, objects, and signs are also "agents." And man, just like the machine, is a hybrid, in other words, a "bifaceted subject-object."

Capitalism is above all a social machine, a megamachine (Mumford), in which, between the human and the non-human, between man and machine, between the organism and technique, there are, rather than an "ontological iron curtain" separating the object from the subject, recurrences, communication, and reversibility.

If the production of subjectivity is "the most important product" of capitalism (Guattari), it must strongly be emphasized that subjectivity exists for the social machine and the technical machine, and that governmentality is exercised over these machines and subjectivities. The concept of subjectivation is omnipresent in the philosophy of the 1970s, but if one makes short shrift of the social and technical machine and of the relationship it has with human subjectivity, is it really possible to understand its process of production and governance?

Capitalism organizes the production and control of subjectivity (the modern genealogy of morals) by way of two different mechanisms which weave together the individuated subject ("social subjection") and its apparent opposite, desubjectivation ("machinic enslavement"). The hold that capitalism has over subjectivity is therefore twofold. Subjection implies techniques of government that pass through and mobilize representation (political and linguistic), knowledge, discursive and visual practices, etc., producing "subjects of law," "political subjects," as well as "subjects" per se, "selves," and individuals. By producing us as individuated subjects, social subjection assigns us an identity, a gender, a profession, a nationality, and so on. It is a signifying and representational confinement from which no one escapes. In contemporary capitalism, these processes and techniques are fully embodied in "human capital," which makes each one of us a "subject" responsible and guilty for his own "actions" and "behavior." The "free subject," in the sense of "freed" from all personal subordination, is realized in the figure of the entrepreneur of the self and in that of the consumer who chooses "sovereignly" from an infinite array of commodities.

Machinic enslavement, on the other hand, refers to non-representational, operational, diagrammatic techniques that function by exploiting partial, modular, subindividual subjectivities. Enslavement aims at and produces what Deleuze calls the "dividual." Capitalism constructs an enslavement in which humans act in the same way as mechanical parts, constituting "human" components and elements of machinism. For management companies like social networks (Facebook) or research engines (Google), for polling firms, data banks, market studies, marketing firms, and so on, you are not a "subject" but rather a platform for the exchange and transformation of information. Your functions, like those of "technical" components, do no more than make the machine run, provide it with raw material—information. Your representations, your psychology, your consciousness, your interiority, etc., are as a rule unnecessary.

Subjection functions based on the subject/object dichotomy, whereas enslavement does not distinguish the organism from the machine, subject from object, or human from technique. The relationship between human being and machine is radically different in the two cases. In subjection, the relationship is one of use and action. The machine is at once an external object with which the human relates as an "active" subject (worker or user) and a *medium* between two subjects. In enslavement, the relationship is one of "mutual internal communication" between human and machine. Subjection and enslavement, subjectivation and desubjectivation, allow us to expand and enrich but also to modify Foucault's concept of biopower. The concept and practices of govern-mentality change markedly because in order to function they must be situated at the intersection of subjection and enslavement.

The extreme of individualization

Contemporary capitalism pushes social subjection and machinic enslavement to their extreme. We are thus simultaneously subject to this twofold relation of power.

Neoliberalism has its own particular way of manipulating the "relation to the self" (the pro-duction of the subject, of the individual) as it pushes the relation to its paroxysm. The epitome of this is "human capital" (the "entrepreneur of the self"),[5] the purpose of subjection. By making the person capital, the latter exacerbates individualism while it compels him to be evaluated and calibrated according to the logic of losses and gains, supply and demand, investment (in education, individual insurance, etc.), and profitability.

The post-Fordist system endlessly solicits the individual, who, thanks to his "freedom" and "autonomy," must continuously arbitrate not only between external situations but also himself. The independent worker, whose model has been imported from salaried work, functions like an individual enterprise and must ceaselessly negotiate between his *economic* "ego" and "superego" precisely because he is responsible for his own fate ("Should I work or should I take a vacation? Should I turn on my phone and make myself available to even the most meager offer of work or should I turn it off and make myself unavailable?" etc.). Isolated by "freedom" itself, the individual is forced to compete not only with others but also with himself. The permanent negotiation with oneself is the form of subjectivation and control specific to neoliberal societies. Just as in the Fordist system, the norm remains external, it is still produced by the socioeconomic system, but everything occurs as if the norm originated in the individual, as if it came solely from the individual.

The order and command must appear to issue from the subject, because "you're in control!" because "you're your own boss!" because "you're your own manager!" Contemporary subjection subjects the individual to "infinite" evaluation and makes the subject his own primary judge. The injunction to be a subject, to give oneself orders, to negotiate permanently with oneself, to obey oneself, is the fulfillment of individualism.

Frustration, resentment, guilt, and fear make up the "passions" of the neoliberal relation to the self, because the promises of self-realization, freedom, and autonomy collide with a reality that systematically nullifies them. The failure of capitalism is not as spectacular as it might be because individualism cancels the failure through the interiorization of the conflict: the "enemy" becomes indistinguishable from a part of the self. "Complaints" are turned against oneself instead of relations of power. Hence the guilt, bad conscience, loneliness, and resentment. The full "sovereignty" of the individual—since the individual is the one who chooses, the one who decides, the one in charge—coincides with his full and complete alienation. Neurosis is the pathology of a bygone capitalism; the "malady" of the twenty-first century manifests itself in "depression": the powerlessness to act, to decide, to undertake projects; passive individual resistance to generalized mobilization, to the injunction to be active, to have plans, to get involved.

Dividuals and the new enslavement

At the same time, neoliberal capitalism pushes desubjectivation to the extreme. The nature and functions of machinic enslavement, which shapes, controls, and governs our behavior by acting on the preindividual components of our subjectivity and on the elementary components of our bodies, strictly depend on the concept of the "machine."

To introduce the concept of the dividual and the techniques that govern it, we must first recognize what machines do in contemporary capitalism. The post-Fordist phase is characterized by a tremendous acceleration of investments in machines, and this involves much more than "production" alone.

Our most "human" actions (speaking, seeing, hearing, reproducing as a "species," feeling, affecting, and being affected, etc.) are today unthinkable without the aid of machines. If capitalists speak of "human capital," it is because nothing "human" escapes machinic enslavements, technical-semiotic assemblages, scientific laboratories and the industries that exploit them. If we are all invariably constituted as "human capital," it is because we are all invariably constituted as component parts, as "inputs" and "outputs" of technical-semiotic networks, including and especially when we are unemployed, in job training, retired, and so on.

Investments in "constant social capital" represent massive investments in "machines," investments on a scale incomparable to the era of industrial capitalism. The expansion of the concept of "constant capital" is justified by the emergence of technical means that correspond to the generalized decoding of flows, a specific feature of post-Fordism. The computer is a machine for instantaneous, generalized decoding; it establishes, structures, and organizes not only production flows but also the flows of communication, images, writing, consumption, and so on, traversing and reconfiguring forms of perception, attention, sensation, vision, and thought. The ubiquitous diffusion of "constant social capital" has created the conditions for a new machinic enslavement and new axiomatics.

Capital is a semiotic operator

The post-Fordist period has been characterized by the deterritorialization of technologies and by the decodification of signs themselves (particularly language). Signs are no longer confined to the signifier/signified dualism but act as "point-signs," "power signs," "asignifying signs," and "operative signs," intervening directly in material flows. Money, stock prices, the spread, algorithms, and scientific equations and formulas constitute semiotics that make the capitalist social machine function in view of both valorization and the *production of subjectivity*, with no need of representation or consciousness. Asignifying semiotics like money might put in play sign systems that have a signifying effect, but their specific function does not involve signification.[6]

Having passed a new threshold of deterritorialization, signs, like the machines they make run, subordinate language to the asignifying semiotics of science and the economy. The effectiveness of language now lies in its capacity to harmonize with the semiotics of money,[7] financial semiotics, algorithms, computer "languages," etc.

In the early 1970s, a poet, a subtle connoisseur of language, proclaimed that we had entered "a period in history in which verbal language is completely conventional and empty (technicized) and the language of behavior (physical and imitative) is of decisive importance." Today our culture expresses itself primarily through the latter, "plus a certain quantity—utterly conventional and extremely impoverished—of verbal language."[8] Contrary, then, to what adherents of the linguistic turn and Lacanians might think, language does not play a central role in post-Fordist capitalism. Like communications and consumption, production does not act on subjectivity primarily or exclusively through language. "The fever to consume is a fever to obey an unspoken command."[9] Unspoken linguistically, although communicated through many other semiotics which, bypassing "expressed ideas" or "consciously expressed values," act directly on the "existential," the "lived." The "ideological barrage," even in a "spoken" media like television, does not involve speech, "it is entirely in things, totally indirect."[10] The system of "physio-imitative" signs is exploited above all by advertising, whose efficacy does not stem from "discursive" and "ideological force" but from the ability to draw on and stick to the semiotics of the world (the "language of things," as Pasolini says). Guattari likewise underscores that:

> Children and adolescents do not learn who they are, at least predominantly, in terms of signifying discourse. They have recourse to what I call asignifying forms of discursivity—music, clothing, the body, behavior—to signs of recognition and to all kinds of machinic systems.[11]

A subjective fact is always generated by an assemblage with multiple heterogeneous semiotic levels, whereas in enslavement linguistic semiotics lose the primacy that structuralism has always attributed to them.

Indexation processes

The double deterritorialization of technical machines and signs constitutes a new axiomatics of decoded flows that permits a new type of measurement and a new type of evaluation.

Signs perform the indexation and symbolization of every "productive" and social activity. Indexes and symbols carry out "codification" that enables the measurement, control, and capture of valorization. The deterritorialization of machines and signs makes the quantification of what was considered non-quantifiable possible (opinions, affects, attention, tastes, social temporalities, etc.). The apparatuses of indexation and symbolization extend from the mathematical notation of financial asset prices to "social networks," in which, through very simple indexes and symbols, such as the famous Facebook "like," evaluation, measurement, hierarchization, and quantification operate.[12] Financial and monetary signs form a higher (more deterritorialized) level of indexation, evaluation, and measurement capable of functioning as a management and capture apparatus of all types of activity (labor, communications, services, consumption, etc.).

Everything becomes measurable and evaluable, not according to the law of labor-value, but according to multiple principles of evaluation at once objective (through digital technologies, signs/indexes and their algebraic syntaxes) and subjective (through the "political" technologies of evaluation that have entered every area of life). Finance/money is imposed as the "measure of measures," capitalizing the valorization differentials of different activities. What one calls "algotrading" (algorithmic trading) is the latest semiotic technique for translating the political power of finance into operations of indexation, evaluation, measurement, and capture.

Capital cannot be reduced to an economic category because it operates as a semiotic power transversal to different levels of production, to different stratifications of power, and to a multiplicity of social intervention of semiotic and machinic elements. The continual accumulation of constant "social" capital and the growing complexity of signs that enables accumulation have taken control of relationships, behavior, opinions, and desires, affecting much more than "paid labor."

The dividual: the deterritorialization of the individual

The twofold deterritorialization of machines and signs, of technologies and "languages," their diffusion as "constant social capital," defines a new machinic enslavement that acts powerfully on subjectivity by undoing the union of individuals and masses proper to disciplinary societies. In control societies, individuals become "dividuals" and populations become surveys, data, markets, or "banks" (Deleuze). The dividual represents a deterritorialization of the individual, while data banks, surveys, market studies, and so on constitute forms of his "collective" existence. The dividual involves a specific type of governance that requires us to consider the concepts of "biopolitics" and "biopower" in light of the technical-semiotic production of subjectivities.

If the individual is, as the term indicates, indivisible, "undividable," because he holds in synthesis, in a "whole" (the ego), the partial, modular, pre-individual subjectivities of which he is composed, the "dividual," by undoing subjective synthesis, is infinitely divisible, infinitely dividable, that is, infinitely composable and, therefore, infinitely "amenable." Deterritorialization decomposes the individual into his constitutive elements (memory, perception, intelligence, feelings, etc.), just as science disaggregates material into its chemical and atomic elements, assigning them their specific functions and potentialities.

The governmentality of enslavement is exercised not on subjectivity as a unity or synthesis but on the human and non-human vectors of subjectivation that traverse subjectivity as well as on the somatic, biological, genetic, and neural components that compose the body. Technologies dissect human senses (sight, hearing, touch, smell, taste) and recompose them in view of producing a subjectivity such that "consumption for consumption's sake" can fulfill and enact that other law of capitalism, "production for production's sake."[13]

Deterritorialization produces a new plasticity in "psychic" and "bodily" subjectivity, a new and formidable capacity to intervene in the "body" and "soul." Ripping apart the "whole" that contained partial and modular subjectivities, the multiplicity of vectors of subjectivation is at once freed from the hold of the individuated subject and captured, subordinated, put "to work," by consumer and communications industries, by pharmaceuticals, drugs, sex, and so on. Pre-individual vectors of subjectivation emit "information," "signals," that interest corporations devoted to consumption and communications. The media and culture industries act on "modules" of subjectivity, while other enormous industrial conglomerates exploit scientific research and technological innovations, intervening in the chemical, genetic, and neural elements of the body. The deterritorialization of the individual provides the basic elements for reconstructing not only "subjects" but also *consumers, voters, communicators*, for building *sexual identities, behavior, appropriate conduct*, and new *corporalities*.

Foucault draws on the neoliberal economist Gary Becker to give a definition of the subjectivity of *homo economicus* that aligns with certain aspects of the definition of the "dividual." Neoliberal *homo economicus*, "human capital," is radically different from classical *homo economicus*, for he is no longer an "atom of freedom," "indivisible," the "intangible partner of laissez-faire." As a "dividual," he is now "divisible," even infinitely divisible, in other words, decomposable into partial and modular subjectivities and into multiple pre-individual vectors of subjectivation. He is therefore "manipulable" and "eminently governable." Inserted into a "milieu," his conformist conduct consists in responding to variations artificially introduced into the environment such that he then appears as the "correlate of a governmentality which will act on the environment and systematically modify its variables."[14] These "environmental" technologies, like enslavement, do not lead to interiorization. According to Foucault, governmental security interventions do not involve "internal subjection." Instead of applying directly to the individual, they act on the "milieu," they define a framework encompassing the individual while leaving enough room for him to "play."

Unlike disciplines, this new governmentality operates in an open space and in a non-chronological temporality, because it "tr[ies] to plan a milieu in terms of events or series of events or possible elements."[15] Governmentality refers to the "temporal and uncertain"; its "security" techniques consist in preventing, anticipating (or even simulating), what will happen. Security governmentality can be described as a cybernetic, modular, and distributive version of power that self-regulates through feedback loops with a subjectivity that has lost the status of the "free" and "autonomous" subject it had in classical liberalism.

One last remark from Foucault seems to me particularly important here. The new *homo economicus*, divisible and without "interiority," constitutes a "contact of surface between the individual and [...] power"; it functions as an "interface" between subjectivities and governmentality. This "does not mean that the whole subject is considered as *homo economicus*," but only that certain modular elements of subjectivity are mobilized toward that end.[16] Power does not act directly on the individual but on "surfaces of contact" which in turn contribute to the processes constitutive of subjectivity.

The different "interfaces" produced by "polling," "ratings," "taste" and "opinion" surveys; the "profiles" constructed by businesses that manage social networks and large data banks (big data);[17] and the models of behavior conveyed by advertising and subjective prototypes[18] make up the phantasmagoria of governmentality techniques which accompany and complement state action. While engaging the individual's subjectivity in various ways and making it, literally, fluctuate, "surfaces of contact" translate subjective conducts into the sign and information flows that capitalist axiomatics and power need in order to assure valorization, control, and domination.[19]

Interfaces are at once apparatuses for inciting and soliciting subjectivity (social subjection) and instruments for indexing, evaluating, and measuring that same subjectivity (machinic enslavement). In other words, economic valorization and the production of subjectivity go hand in hand and partake of the same apparatuses.

Making the body

One can perhaps most clearly grasp the changes in governmentality and its techniques by way of the body. Guattari already warns us that it is not at all obvious that we have a body, that an individual body, a natural body, exists. On the contrary, the body is manufactured and assigned to us. We are assigned a body capable of developing within a social, productive, and domestic space. There are other anthropological systems that do not involve a natural, individual body. In archaic societies, the body is always the subset of a social body, "produced" by marks, tattoos, inscriptions, signs of initiation, and so on. This body does not possess individuated organs and is itself traversed by the souls and spirits that belong to the entire collective.

One of the major initiatory phases of capitalist flows consists in the interiorization of the "natural" body, of the "individuated" body, already structured according to the dualisms of masculine and feminine, soul and body, individual and collective. The production of subjectivity calls for work on the body (first the body, says Nietzsche, and the rest will follow). We can understand how social subjection and machinic enslavement function by looking at the pharmaco-pornographic capitalism very incisively described by Beatriz Preciado.[20] In the creation of gender, sexuality, and sexual identity, interventions on the body occur at the junction of two apparatuses, such that governmentality is exercised at once on the individual and on the dividual. Social subjection engages bodies through the disciplinary techniques of temporal and spatial organization as well as through laws, specialized knowledge, norms, linguistic and visual semiotics, and the education system, just as Foucault demonstrated. Yet this type of power relation does not exhaust the modalities of action and control over the body.

What the state and private enterprise mobilize at the same time is a "material production of the feminine" by utilizing what is most abstract, most deterritorialized: scientific equations, the "power-signs" of chemistry, the "point particles" of the neurosciences, of molecular biology and genetics, acting directly on the body without involving representation or consciousness.

Machinic enslavement entails a normalization that bypasses the norm to engage the activities of chemical, genetic, or neural "programs" or "diagrams," the work of synthetic molecules on real molecules, synthetic hormones on real hormones. It is literally a matter of "molecular," "endocrinological and high-tech" power, exceeding the representational, discursive, and moral techniques that act on the individual/subject.

Social control is exercised through the body but by marking it from the "inside" (by swallowing pills, we swallow power, Preciado says). Through the widespread administration of synthetic hormones (estrogen) into women's bodies, we "produce and reproduce femininity in a pure state," just as the same hormones eliminated by urine are filtered in purifying stations to end up in rivers where they lead to the feminization of fish (male fish that produce eggs[21]).

The force and specificity of capitalism lie less in the performative, in the symbolic, or in speech—all techniques common to every form of power—than in the forms of operative "diagrammatic" action that do not involve consciousness or representation. Our body is marked by the power-signs, the asignifying signs, produced in the laboratories of the pharmaceutical industry and genetics. They do not apply to the "subject" as a whole but to its subindividual, "biological," chemical, and atomic constituents in view of creating a new "body" and a new "subject" according to the demands of production and reproduction of capital. Machinic enslavement creates a subject that no longer reflects, that is no longer conscious or a product of "intersubjectivity": "In opposition to the Freudian archeology of the ego appears a hormonal, electrochemical, media-related, and ultraconnected subject."[22]

Social subjection and machinic enslavement are not the monopoly of the state. Since the 1920s, control of these apparatuses by private enterprise has constantly expanded in order to ensure the operations of "state capitalism." In capitalism, at least since the start of the last century, the population is not taken in hand by the state alone. In certain passages of *Security, Territory, Population*, Foucault makes of the space extending from the population to the public the field in which governmentality intervenes. But while the population and its biological "needs" have diversified and grown (particularly with regard to welfare services), what he calls "public" has multiplied exponentially. The press, radio, cinema, and television publics have now diversified into Internet and social-network users. The latter are no longer, strictly speaking, a public. The "population" is continually translated, channeled, and solicited in real time into ratings, polls, and market surveys; every type and variety of statistics take its pulse. Is there anything more effective for controlling the conduct of "human beings" than consumption and the techniques of media and communications?

Technophobes and technophiles

There are those who disregard machines and technology; then there are technophobes and technophiles, who invest them with a power they do not possess. With each technological breakthrough (the web, algorithms, bitcoin, big data, smart cities, etc.), machines and technology are imbued with utopian hopes of liberation and apocalyptic fears of domination. These contradictory sentiments arise with desperate regularity because the relationship between technology and power (the power of capital) has been poorly formulated.

For Gilbert Simondon and Félix Guattari machines are not synonymous with capital and power; they are neither neutral nor simply means to an end. They have a specific ontological consistency which "labor" and "capital" tend to obscure and instrumentalize. Simondon considers the machine to be more than a tool but less than a slave. The most powerful computational machines, equipped with the most powerful algorithms, "do not have the same degree of reality as an ignorant slave." The slave can revolt. Of course, more than their mere disruption, revolt implies a profound transformation of purpose-driven conducts. The machine may malfunction but it cannot revolt, it cannot change its purpose over the course of its existence, in other words, for Simondon, it is not "self-creating." The machine (automatic or cybernetic) adapts and regulates itself according to a predetermined objective, whereas human beings are capable of self-creation, transforming themselves in sudden leaps and ruptures (subjective conversion).

Francisco Varela distinguishes between auto-poietic machines, which engender their own organization, and allopoietic machines, which produce something other than themselves. He places technological machines in the second category. According to Guattari, however, the latter are always vicariously autopoietic because always necessarily in relation with autopoietic machines, that is, with humans. Only abstraction allows us to separate the man-machine assemblage, because human and non-human always accompany one another. Yet the human-non-human relation can be configured in multiple ways, for it is the product of a social machine, of its universes of values and its worlds.

To grasp the relationship between technology and power, one has to distinguish between the technical machine and the social machine and recognize that the latter is always political. Algorithms, though widely used by finance capital, did not provoke the subprime crisis. Algorithms are programmed to buy a stock at the lowest price and sell it at the highest, but they did not establish the "laws" of capital valorization, the infinite quest for profit, competition, and so on. Computational machines might accelerate the capitalist social machine, bolster the repetitive function of production, consumption, and appropriation through technological automatism, but there is a difference in nature between the two types of repetition. The changes in axioms that took place during the transition from Fordism to neoliberalism or during the 2007 crisis and its "governance" (austerity, reduced state budgets, etc.) derive not from algorithms but from the capitalist social machine and, therefore, from a specific politics.

Digital machines increase productivity by replacing human labor, yet they do not produce unemployment. The crisis and unemployment are categories and policies of capital, in no way those of machines. Likewise, "liberation" is not an effect of technology because, according to Simondon, machines must themselves be "liberated" through the invention of a social machine capable of breaking the hold which the logics of capital and labor exercise over them.

Cybernetic machines establish modular, diffuse, and decentered functions, a "technological" microphysics of production, consumption, and governmentality. They do more than record, stock, and transmit information; they constitute platforms for self-regulation and retroaction over the economy, the social sphere, and subjectivity. Yet it is always axiomatics, the capitalist social machine, that defines and limits them. Axiomatics, such as we have seen it at work during the crisis, easily changes the modalities in which governmentality is exercised by (re)centralizing the power distributed and by using the technological environment and its modularity to assure and affirm the primacy of property over any other "end." The capitalist social machine allows "intellectuals" and "artists" (and any one at all) to invent and create—it even encourages them. But it is always axiomatics, in other words, politics, that selects, chooses, hierarchizes, and articulates scientific and technological inventions.

Constructing a technical object involves creating "availability" so that "the newly detachable technical object can be grouped with other technical objects according to various ensembles [...]. The industrial ensemble is not the only one that it is possible to construct with technical objects: nonproductive ensembles can also be made."[23] What determines a given ensemble? The social machine, by integrating the universe of technological machines into a multiplicity of other "universes" (economic, social, political, sexual, semiotic, etc.). And how does the machine work? By processing flows of a completely different order (those of labor, technology, money, gender, subjectivity, signs, etc.). It divides and organizes them employing "techniques" that function neither on information nor on energy (mechanical or thermodynamic).

This is another, more fundamental reason not to confuse the social machine with the technical machine. "The technical being can only be defined in terms of information and the transformation of different types of energy and information."[24] Cybernetics enlarges this definition in positing that "any organism is held together [...] by the possession of means for the acquisition, use, retention, and transmission of information."[25] The social machine is not reducible to information and energy. The latter represent simply the actualized dimension of the assemblage. In order to produce commodities and profit, the capitalist social machine must first be able to produce a world and its universes of values, desires, and its existential territories, however impoverished or loathsome they may be. The social machine, like the real, is not only constituted by the present state of affairs but also by the systems of possibility and impossibility which are not governed by the laws of science.

Semiotic and linguistic flows, just like material, social, economic, etc., flows, exist within actualized spatiotemporal coordinates, whereas the forces of "self-affirmation," the source of "universes of values," of "existential territories," of the possible and impossible, represent the intensive, incorporeal dimension of the social machine that lies outside ordinary space and time coordinates. Eluding determination and physical causality, the incorporeal constitutes a non-energetic and non-informational "machinism."

The transformations and ruptures that occur in subjectivities, existence, and society are first of all incorporeal. Intelligence, technology, and science have not failed us, the creation of new possibilities and desires has. Utopians and doomsayers neglect the fact that the man-machine relation is always bound to a social machine, to a capitalist axiomatics or a war machine, in other words, to a politics of possibility and impossibility.

Subjection and enslavement in the crisis

The debt crisis allows us to enlarge the array of techniques of governmentality described by Foucault, and especially to specify the political strategy of capitalism, introducing what seems to lack in his analysis of neoliberalism—namely, the capitalist relation.

If Foucault perfectly understands the discontinuities separating security societies from disciplinary societies, he neglects the continuity of the capitalist relation, which, despite its profound changes, remains grounded in the class differences it reproduces at the social and worldwide levels. For it is indeed "capital" that has imposed new axioms. The crisis has put the French philosopher's—and the Marxist—toolbox in disarray, for rather than adhering to the capital-labor relation, it has revealed the opposition between creditors and debtors. After holding center stage since the beginning of capitalism, industrial capital and the two classes it encompasses (capitalists and workers) has now given way to forms of production, the market, and conflicts based in financialization. This is something radically new.

The relation between creditors and debtors has come to the fore in the debt crisis, even if it has been at the heart of neoliberal capitalist policies from the beginning. The creditor-debtor relation assured and oriented the turn from Fordism to post-Fordism, and it is the same relation that has incited, solicited, and shaped globalization. It represents a shift and a disruption in macropolitical power relations insofar as it subordinates the capital-labor relation to its own logic without eliminating it, indeed, extending it to the entire planet. The change has left the workers' movement with no voice and no political weapons (in fact, it is the movement's death knell).

It is not democracy, as Mario Tronti thought, but a completely new capitalist relation that has ultimately undermined the workers' movement and, simultaneously, democracy. No one clearly understood the transition carried out by financial deterritorialization (money as capital), and certainly not Foucault, who totally neglected the role of money and of money as capital in his work on neoliberalism. He recognized that individualizing governmentality, encompassing "disciplinary control (*quadrillage*), unlimited regulation, subordination/ classification, the norm,"[26] was thoroughly in decline. Today, however, the "general normalization and exclusion of those who cannot be normalized" specific to disciplinary societies are no longer required, since it is now a matter of controlling and making the entirety of the population productive within the space opened by techniques of "optimization of systems of difference."[27] Governmentality must act on a society "in which the field is left open to fluctuating processes, in which minority individuals and practices are tolerated."[28] In the debt crisis, these techniques of differentiation function at full capacity, and yet they restrict subjects' freedom instead of producing it by neutralizing rather than increasing the ability to make decisions, by tolerating the interests of capital alone.

The intensification of the crisis caused by the debts of private enterprise, banks, and states has exacerbated both social subjection and machinic enslavement, pushing the logic of the individual and that of the dividual to their extreme. In the crisis, the population must fluctuate like stock-market prices; it must rise and fall following the variations of the spread. On the one hand, we are constructed as "subjects," assigned to our "nature" as responsible and guilty individuals (guilty for indebtedness). We must interiorize this responsibility and guilt and assume the consequences by atoning for our faults, paying and reimbursing our creditors. On the other hand, we are instituted as "dividuals" into elements, parts, cogs, of the "debtmachine." "Dividuals" must do no more than "respond" to the signals emitted by the spread, adapt in real time to the variations of the new circumstances of austerity and recession. Fluctuations in debt flows have a direct and instantaneous effect on our way of life. The spread constitutes the interface between governmentality and the governed, the surface of contact between power and the population. While representational semiotics endow us with a memory, consciousness, and speech capable of promising and keeping the promise to reimburse a debt into which we have never entered, the asignifying signs of the stock market and spread act on *homo economicus* by calling upon his essential characteristic, his "responsiveness," precisely as Foucault said.

Foucault's observation that governmentality is "environmental," that is, capable of creating a milieu compelling one to respond "automatically" to systemic variations, is crucial. But we must nonetheless emphasize that if governmentality completes the transformation of *homo economicus* into a dividual, it also maximizes his subjection, the constitution of a responsible and guilty individual. The two processes of subjection and enslavement are coextensive; we are caught up in one no less than in the other.

The sovereign, disciplinary, and security techniques of governmentality always function and are always deployed together, but the intensification of the crisis and of its axioms brings to the fore the first two, even if the third persists. State sovereignty is mobilized uniquely over the population, since sovereignty over the economy has in part been neutralized first by ordoliberalism then, more radically, by neoliberalism. Disciplinary technologies, which have never disappeared, acquire a new importance, particularly in the management of the "unemployed," the "poor," the labor market, and in the governance of social services. Facing no organized resistance, the authoritarianism of our declining democracies is founded on the articulation of these three forms of power.

REREADING LENIN:

THE PAST AND PRESENT OF FINANCE CAPITAL

Can we separate the "real" economy from the "virtual" economy, industrial and commercial capital from finance capital? Is it possible to conceive of the economic cycle of capital as a passage from material accumulation to financial accumulation (Giovanni Arrighi)? Is finance capital specific to the present era? Is it the monetary expression of the cognitive economy, of the information and knowledge society (El Mouhoub Mouhoud), or is it degeneration, an "excess," an anomaly of industrial capital and its ethics of labor and effort?

A reading of Lenin's *Imperialism, the Highest Stage of Capitalism* and of the economic literature it draws on allows us to redefine the concept of capital and to periodize capitalist development in light of the "hegemonic" function of finance capital. Indeed, capital is not confined to industrial and commercial capitalism; it encompasses finance capital as its endpoint, which alone gives it unity and coherence by constituting capitalism as an integral whole. Consequently, the formula of finance capital (M–M') represents the "purest" form of the capitalist dynamic, that of money that self-valorizes by appropriating all forms of value.

Thanks to Lenin's work, we can define two major phases in the domination of finance capital, covering the world wars, the European civil wars, the 1929 crisis, the New Deal, the "Trente Glorieuses" (1945–1975), and the cold war. The first runs from 1870 to 1914, during which, *for the first time*, the complete process of capital developed—including industrial, commercial, and finance capital—in conformity with the exigencies of finance capital. The second began in the 1970s, after which it would no longer be a question of hegemony but of a total reconfiguration of the planet by finance capital and its axiomatics. Between these two phases, the Fordist-Keynesian period appears rather like a political-economic exception characterized in particular by the neutralization of the political power of finance capital. The latter was reduced to the simple "economic" function of financing an industrial capital "administered" according to a political compromise between capitalists and trade unions overseen by the state.[1]

Imperialism as finance capital

Lenin defines imperialism as "the epoch of finance capital and of monopolies."[2] Against Kautsky, for whom "imperialism is a product of highly developed industrial capitalism" in which railroads represent the ultimate product of capitalist industry's main sectors (the iron, steel, and mining industries), Lenin argues that "the definition is of no use at all" because "the characteristic feature of imperialism is *not* industrial *but* finance capital."[3]

The hegemony of finance capital is not an anomaly of capitalism. On the contrary, it completes the cycle of capital. The "self-movement" of the valorizing process of money that Marx described theoretically does not occur practically until finance capital has taken on a certain consistency. Lenin interprets finance capital as "a personal link-up, so to speak [...], between banks and the biggest industrial and commercial enterprises" such that "a handful of monopolists subordinate to their will all the operations, both commercial and industrial, of the whole of capitalist society."[4]

Rudolf Hilferding provides a more rigorous definition. With finance capital, "all partial forms of capital are brought together" in a coherent whole organized according to the laws of capital's infinite valorization. "Finance capital has the appearance of money capital, and its form of development is indeed that of money which yields money (M–M′)—the most general and inscrutable form of the movement of capital."[5]

The transition from the M–C–M′ form of industrial capital to a still more deterritorialized form, M–M′, is therefore nothing new, and all those who continue to separate "healthy" industrial capital from "perverse" or morally reprehensible finance capital perpetuate the misunderstanding. Capital's aim is not production but valorization, and the purpose of valorization is appropriation. Production is nothing if it fails to ensure the realization of the formula M–M′.

Property

A new hegemonic form of property emerges in the same way. Finance capital generalizes and renders irreversible the split between "property" and the management of production. The nature of property, which is moreover no longer directly linked to the means of production, as it was for Marx, appears in its purest form in the stock market: Property ceases to express any specific relation of production and becomes a claim to the yield, apparently unconnected with any particular activity.[6]

"All property is capital," Hilferding argues. "Debts are also capital, as every state loan demonstrates. All capital is equal, and is embodied in those printed certificates which rise and fall in value on the stock exchange."[7] Instead of disputing the appropriation of industrial capital, stock-market property is the most adequate and the most general manifestation of capitalist appropriation. At the turn of the twentieth century, we witness "immense progress in the socialization of production. In particular, the process of technical invention and improvement becomes socialized. [...] Production becomes social, but appropriation remains private," made up in large part of rent.[8]

Rentiers and the collective capitalist

The subjective condition of this "new capitalism" is the rentiers and financiers, who personify the abstract movements of finance capital in the same way as capitalists and workers personify the movements of industrial capital: "the supremacy of finance capital over all other forms of capital means the predominance of the rentier and of the financial oligarchy."[9] Finance capital, like industrial capital, constitutes a relation of power. If rentiers and creditors are one term of the relation, debtors represent the other. The creditor-debtor relation is evoked in Lenin's analyses[10] as well as in those of the authors he cites, but it concerns only relations among states and power relations among capitalists.

Lenin's analysis has several weak points, notably concerning the role of the stock market. Lenin believes that the stock market will vanish with the disappearance of free competition and the establishment of monopolies. For Hilferding, on the other hand, the stock market fulfills a fundamental function, as it would later for Keynes: to make money liquid, to make capital immediately available. The "immense" tying-up of capital in big industry calls for an institution capable of making money liquid and, therefore, mobile. The "renaissance of finance capital" in the late 1970s does not simply mean a renaissance of speculation and rent. The renaissance of "capital" in its most "general" and abstract form would occur under the aegis of the stock market and the financial institutions which together multiply the mechanisms designed to make capital liquid.

Although Lenin's "economic" analysis presents certain weaknesses, it nonetheless makes a fundamental political point. Banks, it would seem, "transact[...] a purely technical and exclusively auxiliary operation," and yet in reality they do more than concentrate immense amounts of capital; they also centralize information and knowledge throughout the production cycle—information and knowledge unavailable to individual capitalists. This "handful of monopolists" "are enabled—by means of their banking connections, their current accounts and other financial operations—first, to *ascertain exactly* the financial position of the various capitalists, then to *control* them, […] and finally to *entirely determine* their fate."[11] In the "new capitalism," finance capital, far from simply embodying predation and greed, represents the "collective capitalist," the site of command of the world market and of the recomposition of the capitalist class.

The periodization of capitalism

The dates are very important. With all the authors he cites, Lenin agrees that the transition from the "old capitalism" to the "new capitalism" took place around 1860–1870. At the moment Marx publishes Book One of *Capital*, the valorization process appears in its entirety for the first time governed by finance capitalism (this is why Lenin speaks of a "new capitalism"). In Marx's time, finance was still at its very first stage of development, and his analyses could only be based on the concept rather than the reality of "money," even if his New York *Tribune* articles from the 1850s show that he foresaw the power of finance.[12] Book Three of *Capital*, in which Marx analyzes credit money, is in fact a series of scattered notes. Engels, who collected and organized them, indicates in a footnote that Marx could not have known of the changes the system was undergoing in the late 1880s and 1890s, changes that were turning the global market into an effective reality. From then on, therefore, capitalism would look profoundly different from the Marxist description.

The advent of this "new capitalism" requires that one distinguish between finance and finance capital. Finance can be found among Genoese bankers as well as in seventeenth-century Holland without there being an actual cycle of capital (the capitalist process as Marx understood it). As of the 1970s one can no longer interpret capitalist phases as a succession and transition from material accumulation to financial accumulation, as Arrighi does, since the capital cycle, the union of the three forms of capital, has been fully established. The neoliberal sequence is still more conclusive, for it begins (and ends or will end) with finance capital, which commands and directs the new industrialization and the international division of labor. It is thus pointless to seek out a new hegemon founded on material production.[13] Financialization does not come after industrial capitalism, it precedes and coincides with it. This includes China, a country whose development has taken place during a more or less cordial "entente" with the United States according to a new international division of labor dominated by the owners of capital.

The speed with which capitalism transformed from Keynesian-Fordism to neoliberalism left its opponents powerless, reformists and revolutionaries alike. To try to follow the transformation by analyzing "labor" or technological innovations was not a bad idea. It was, however, insufficient: capital asserts the rediscovered hegemony of finance capital. But this time the latter is armed with especially effective mechanisms for intervention. Designed to control the destructive power of M–M' unleashed as of 1914, these mechanisms would paradoxically help to reconstruct the same dynamic.

One of the most insightful specialists of money for Marx, the economist Suzanne de Brunhoff, considers the hegemony of finance capital as "temporary." Yet it was the hegemony of the industrial capital of the great Fordist corporations that represented a completely exceptional and unrepeatable parenthesis in the history of capitalism. The political misunderstanding that Mario Tronti[14] speaks of arises not so much because we mistook, in the 1960s and 70s, the dawn of capital with its twilight, but that we did not sufficiently—theoretically or historically—take into account the whole of the capital cycle, whose crowning achievement is finance capital. The analysis of capital cannot be centered on production and its transformations alone (from manufacturing to industry, to big industry and the so-called post-industrial age), for finance capital, which, politically, concludes and controls the process of capital as of 1870, must be accounted for.

Lenin cites the banking specialist Jacob Riesser according to whom "the first avant-garde political confrontations have taken place over finance." Today, much more than in the past, we can affirm that it is over the debtor-creditor relation that capital has chosen to do battle.

Colonialism and the export of capital

The becoming-rent of profit is not a new invention of contemporary capitalism. It is already the reality of the "new capitalism" described by Lenin: "Typical of the old capitalism, when free competition held undivided sway, was the export of goods. Typical of the latest stage of capitalism, when monopolies rule, is the export of *capital*."[15] Indeed, the European imperialist countries of the late nineteenth century are financial countries: a predominant portion of their wealth comes from foreign investments, particularly from their own colonies. "Shortly before the First World War, around 40% of French national wealth came from real-estate investments [...] between a third and a half of these assets were foreign. [...] Only Great Britain did better, where foreign investments in 1907 made up nearly 40% of British national wealth."[16]

A German author cited by Lenin, Schulze-Gaevernitz, makes a very interesting observation that helps to understand credit and debt as a specific power relation. First, he agrees with the diagnostic of most observes of the time: "Great Britain," says Schulze-Gaevernitz, "is gradually becoming transformed from an industrial into a creditor state." Moreover, he argues that the national wealth of England, "rent," was increasing faster than "profit" (in another passage Lenin cites, he quantifies the difference: rent is nine times higher than profit).

> Notwithstanding the absolute increase in industrial output and the export of manufactured goods, there is an increase in the relative importance of income from interest and dividends, issues of securities, commissions and speculation in the whole of the national economy. In my opinion, it is precisely this that forms the economic basis of imperialist ascendency.[17]

But what Schulze-Gaevernitz reintroduces is the creditor-debtor relation as a power relation: "The creditor is more firmly attached to the debtor than the seller is to the buyer," which means that the creditor-debtor relation is more restrictive than the buyer-seller relation. The great novelty of contemporary financialization lies in its expansion of the relation to the whole of society through consumer credit and state sovereign debt. The typical features of finance capital are still the sale, purchase, and insurance of credit/debt, exactly as before the First World War, save for one minor difference—that starting in the 1980s, the credit-debt relation spreads to all types of service (consumption, education, healthcare, pension funds).

In the capitalism of the New Deal and of the "Trente Glorieuses," debt does not stand at the center of political conflict because finance capital as "collective capitalist" has been neutralized. Putting an end to the catastrophe caused by classical liberalism presupposed what Keynes called the "euthanasia of the rentier" and the politically-motivated return to the centrality of the capital-labor relation.

In finance capital, the creditor-debtor relation has a scope and function totally different from those that the capitalist-worker relation had in industrial capital. Its fundamental characteristic is to constitute an apparatus of command and capture not only of industrial labor but also of other forms of production. It is therefore the ideal instrument for dominating and exploiting colonies in which different modes of production coexist (preindustrial, slave-based, commercial, industrial, etc.). Hobson identifies the period from 1884 to 1900 as a moment of intense colonial expansion "most closely connected with the 'latest stage in the development of capitalism,' with finance capital."[18] Finance capital and its "irrational" rationality led to the overexploitation of colonies, for rent had to be paid. The aggression of British imperialism "is explained by the income of £90 million to £100 million from 'invested' capital, the income of the rentiers."[19] Exploitation—and to be more precise, we should speak of predation—was absolutely necessary to the monopolies generated by finance capital: "Colonial possession alone gives the monopolies complete guarantee against all contingencies in the struggle against competitors."[20]

Although the direct territorial occupation characteristic of nineteenth- and early twentieth-century colonialism no longer pertains, today the export of capital is likewise the method for controlling and exploiting the planet. Since finance capital recovered its status of "collective capitalist," the movement of capital determines every country's fate, in particular that of developing countries. The financial crises that have followed one upon the next (especially in Asia and South America), whose number would explode in the 1980s, have their direct origin in the movement of capital toward ever-higher yields. As Brazil, Turkey, and India have recently shown, the economic stability of developing countries is strictly linked to the goodwill of investors. A downtick in Chinese growth affecting other developing countries is enough for capital to flee to the US and certain parts of Europe.

In contemporary capitalism, the creditor-debtor relation, in addition to functioning as a new type of colonialism, represents a form of internal "colonization" of production and of the populations of "Western" countries. "Overexploitation" is integral to the latter's investments, where capital demands returns on the order of 10%, 12%, or 15%. In this context, public debt, what Hilferding unhesitatingly calls capital, reveals itself to be a formidable apparatus of power in the hands of finance capital. The securitization of public debt is the instrument for an immense transfer of wealth from wage-earners and the population toward financial investors. Since the start of the crisis, Europe has thus gone from an average public debt of 66.5% of GDP in 2007 to 90.5% in 2012, allowing creditors to get rich off of the interest. Austerity has not meant the same thing for everyone. Public debt has enabled the recovery and expansion of financial markets (especially in France). It has further demonstrated how well it serves as leverage for "structural reforms," for austerity measures, and for the government of people's behavior.

The market, free competition, and the integration of the working class

For Lenin, industrial monopolies and the concentration of capital in banks are the direct consequences of "free competition." The freedom to produce and trade turns into its opposite, unleashing competition among "imperialisms" and leading to the worst slaughter in history.

The transition from free competition to monopolies is inscribed in the very "nature" of capital. Instead of tending toward "general equilibrium" thanks to the laws of supply and demand, it continually amplifies disequilibriums. For what defines capital is infinite valorization, which has no other purpose than the excess of its own augmentation. Thus, under the aggressive pressures exerted by finance capital, which accomplishes the infinite of accumulation, destructive creation transforms into destruction alone.

Lenin completely grasps the political significance of the dynamic of this "new capitalism." In the imperialist period that he saw firsthand, capital could no longer expand its limits—because of the fall in profit margins—and, therefore, could no longer make its limits the engine of its specific dynamic. On the contrary, they became insurmountable obstacles which could only be overcome through the all-out destruction of fixed capital, variable capital (the labor force), and the society, populations, and "natural" environments they inhabited. The tendency toward crisis and war is inscribed in M–M'. The growth of capital is never peaceful.

Still, what the Marxism of the time underestimated—and this is still the case today—is, on the one hand, capital's capacity to overcome its impasses through the creation of institutions, which, with ordo- and neoliberalism, would produce a "new market," new "free competition," and, above all, a new model for the state. On the other hand, it underestimated the capacity of the working class and the population in general to become integrated into capitalist valorization through mass consumption and welfare.[21]

The fundamental objective of institutional creation is to liberate financial institutions from the grip of capitalist ownership, especially central banks but also the banking system generally, which was at certain points nationalized. Accordingly, these institutions were deprived of the possibility of operating as sites for the recomposition of the capitalist class (the Leninist "collective capitalist"); they were reduced to simple financing structures of industrial capitalism, which had become, through political will, the fundamental political relation. The infinite of valorization was subordinated to an entirely political reproduction based in the capital-labor relation. The recovery of control over financial institutions would be the sine qua non of neoliberalism. It is out of these institutions that the newly recomposed political class would emerge and not via a new form of industrialization (cognitive, cultural, informational, etc., capitalism).

The finance capital of the years 1870–1914 coexisted with a nation-state guaranteeing the former's reterritorialization as well as the aggressive competition among the capital of different nations. It led to the destruction not only of capital in this form but also to that of the nation-state itself. The reconstruction of market functions and free competition by ordoliberals would depend on "Keynesian" interventionist mechanisms, but it would change the meaning and purpose of these mechanisms by creating an integrally economic state. The difference between ordoliberals and neoliberals does not lie in the fact that the latter refuse any kind of state intervention, as if it were possible to return to pre-1870 capitalism, to the "spontaneous" operations of the market, and to free competition. For ordoliberals, the state must aggressively intervene in order to assure the functioning of the market as well as the reproduction of workers and the population according to a logic of "deproletarianization." For neoliberals, the state, although continuing to intervene, must "assist" capital alone, assuring, on the one hand, the distribution of revenue to the advantage of business, creditors, and the wealthiest of the population and, on the other hand, the privatization of all welfare-state services. But what first ordoliberalism then neoliberalism understood was that competition, the market, and business, far from being spontaneous apparatuses, must be "assisted" (and vigorously assisted) by the state and institutions.

In the period beginning in the 1970s, the global market is no longer fragmented into a multiplicity of national imperialisms embroiled in a bitter struggle, as had been the case before the First World War. It is configured, rather, as a polycentric transnational space traversed with tensions, antagonisms, and contradictory interests that manage momentarily to reconcile more or less well. In this configuration, "the integrally economic state" is, given its diminished sovereignty, only one constituent of the power apparatuses that facilitate and guarantee the existence and proliferation of the logic of finance capital (M–M'). The state is no longer able to represent the general interest; on the contrary, it is radically subordinated to financial logic, functioning as a component part of its mechanisms.

No less than the rest of the Marxist tradition, Lenin fails to foresee the integration of the working class and the population into the capitalist economy through increases in wages and income. For the Bolshevik revolutionary, it is impossible for capitalism to "raise the living standards of the masses, who in spite of the amazing technical progress are everywhere still half-starved and poverty-stricken."[22]

The integration of the working class and the population into the logic of valorization would come about, first, through mass consumption (in the US at the beginning of the century and, after the war, in Europe and Japan) and, concomitantly, the advent of the "culture industry," with its ever more sophisticated techniques for the subjective engagement of the consumer, and second, through the establishment of the welfare state.

Yet there were signs that foreshadowed the development. At the end of the nineteenth century, a clear trend began to emerge: laws on workplace accidents in France and Germany, legislation on work hours, laws on workers' pensions, and so on. The remarkable difference with the nineteenth and twentieth centuries is that, at the time, the political defeats the workers' movement inevitably suffered were accompanied by "advances" in social rights (laws on maximum hours, wages, retirement, accidents, etc.). Conversely, today's political defeats run parallel with a decline in social victories, and the new composition of the proletariat remains incapable of imposing new rights. The lesson we can draw from these events accords with Lenin's intuition: the closure of the economic cycle is not economic, à la Quesnay (the interdependence of economic activities), but always political. And this political closure also concerns technique and science, for, as we have seen, contrary to what the technophobes and technophiles believe, it is in fact finance capital that determines the framework and axiomatics within which technique and science operate, and not the reverse.

The construction of the global market

The characteristic traits of the period 1870–1914 reappear in the neoliberal phase although in a very different form, because accumulation and financialization are no longer achieved through nation-state imperialisms; because industrial and commercial capital have become indistinguishable; because financialization permeates and shapes not only industry and services but also society on the whole. The resemblance is not surprising since it is a question of those features specific to the capitalist cycle that are fully realized in finance capital.

Deindustrialization is not a contemporary phenomenon; starting in the 1870s, it is constitutive of the international division of labor carried out by finance capital. The Fordist-Keynesian compromise prevented deindustrialization in the national context, but once the capitalist class was remade to the advantage of finance capital, everything resumed as if the seventy years separating us from the First World War had never happened. Hobson had already spotted the trend in England at the close of the nineteenth century: "The number of rentiers in England is about one million. The percentage of the productively employed population to the total population is declining: 23% in 1851, 15% in 1901."[23] The export of capital entails the renovation of the international division of labor whose course Schulze-Gaevernitz describes: "'Europe will shift the burden of physical toil—first agriculture and mining, then the rougher work in industry—on to the colored races, and itself be content with the role of the rentier.'"[24] And, Hobson reminds us, this phenomenon accelerated with the division of China among imperialist powers.

> The greater part of Western Europe might then assume the appearance and character already exhibited by tracts of country in the South of England, in the Riviera, and in the tourist-ridden or residential parts of Italy and Switzerland, little clusters of wealthy aristocrats drawing dividends and pensions from the Far East, with a somewhat larger group of professional retainers and tradesmen and a larger body of personal servants and workers in the transport trade and in the final stages of production of the more perishable goods; all the main arterial industries would have disappeared, the staple foods and manufactures flowing in as tribute from Asia and Africa.[25]

The foresight is extraordinarily lucid. What he could not foresee was that Chinese industrialization would take place in collaboration with and under the direction of a communist party. But the description of heads of state as "functionaries" of finance capital and of industrialists and merchants as its "employees" is faultless and seems to have been written thirty years ago. Hobson advises those who doubt that China might become the factory of the world to consider

> the vast extension of such a system which might be rendered feasible by the subjection of China to the economic control of similar groups of financiers, investors, and political and business officials, draining the greatest potential reservoir of profit the world has ever known, in order to consume it in Europe. The situation is far too complex, the play of world forces far too incalculable, to render this or any other single interpretation of the future very probable; but the influences which govern the imperialism of Western Europe today are moving in this direction, and, unless counteracted or diverted, make towards some such consummation.[26]

As Lenin remarks, the author is perfectly correct.

Finance capital, in the past and presently, has systematically worked toward and succeeded in establishing a division between the "higher stratum" of wage-earners and the "lower, strictly speaking proletarian, stratum" within "capitalist" countries. It seeks to create "privileged categories" among workers and to separate them from the great mass of the proletariat. The proletariat's adoption of middle-class attitudes—a theme that is not only Pasolini's or Agamben's but had already been advanced by Engels and again by Lenin—has grown much more widespread than in the late nineteenth century. Today's financial oligarchy establishes a new division and a more vigorous "collaboration" with trade unions, particularly with those that manage pension funds. Paradoxically, the financialization of society has been accomplished with the accumulated money of pensions. As a consequence, the integration of the working class and the population in general is not only the result of mass consumption and the powerful culture industry; it not only operates through the welfare state, but also with the participation of a minority of wage-earners with a stake in financial revenue through pension funds.

While at the turn of the twentieth century "'the problem of unemployment [was] mainly a London problem and that of the lower stratum, *to which the politicians attach little importance*,'"[27] and while unemployment had only a marginal role in Fordism, it is now a mass phenomenon. In contemporary finance capital, Keynesian unemployment policies have been transformed, with the complicity of unions and parties of the "left," into policies for the creation and maintenance of unemployment and of the expanding number of poor workers.

Confronted with the international division of imperialist labor that had established deep divisions among the exploited, revolutionary internationalism arose and, unlike what happens today, fought against laws restricting immigration, imposing trade tariffs, and protecting wage differences between nationals and foreigners. That kind of worker chauvinism could only lead, as we can clearly see today, to a war among the poor.

> European trade unions nonetheless resisted the pressure to control immigration, even when it came from their own membership; instead they proposed measures designed to protect wages, to increase the wages of foreigners, and to prevent employers from underpaying them. The unions did not answer the grievances of their membership by excluding foreigners but by integrating them into the system and raising everyone up.[28]

The financialization of the West is still more thorough than during the period 1870–1914. England, for example, was a financial state at the time of imperialism. What is remarkably new is that today it is the largest tax haven in the world. The rich and corporations, even from countries subject to austerity measures (rich Italians, Spanish, and Greeks), continue to buy real estate and make their deposits there because of the constant rises in value brought about by the "crisis." The markets for real-estate and financial "services" (in other words, tax havens) that caused the crisis are now the bases for "new" growth, which—and this is the central problem—will inevitably throw us back into an intensified crisis whose consequences we can only imagine. The "recovery" of British growth is proportional to the blindness of our neoliberal elites.

Just as in the imperialist era, contemporary democracy has been circumvented by techniques of transnational governmentality, whose active basis lies in finance capital: "Once the supreme management of the German banks has been entrusted to the hands of a dozen persons, their activity is even today more significant for the public good than that of the majority of Ministers of State."[29] The authoritarian governance established everywhere following the subprime crisis will be forced to radicalize since "growth" and economic stability are not foregone conclusions. Recession and stagnation are more probable than renewed growth, as Japan has demonstrated over the last twenty years. In any event, the finance capital's logic of destructive valorization, which has not been subject to any effective control, will again undermine the already weak foundations for this improbable "exit" from the crisis.

From this point of view, Greece is not an exceptional case; it is a laboratory in which the resistance of a population to authoritarian governance can be measured. It could very well represent the future of our democracies. The convulsions of the capitalist cycle provoked by finance capital call for a reactionary economic as well as political, social, and ideological reterritorialization. A process that in Europe is occurring surprisingly fast.

Today we find the same levels of appropriation of wealth and the same class differentials (inequalities) as in the period of finance capital's first hegemony. The symmetry between the two phases is troubling. In the US before the 1929 crisis, "according to tax statistics, which tend to underestimate high incomes, the top 1% of the population with the highest incomes received around 16% of total income; the richest 1% held 37% of the wealth of the entire country." Over the course of the "Trente Glorieuses," the share of income of the top 1% in France went from 16% to 8%. Everything changed with neoliberalism: in twenty years, the share went back from 8% to 16%.[30]

Among the other "curiosities" one finds in Lenin's book, the authors of the time describe an "ideological" environment that should be familiar to us. Gerhard Hildebrand, a Marxist turned social-democrat, calls for "the construction of a United States of Western Europe (without Russia) to carry out common action [...] against the Blacks of Africa," against the "great Islamic movement," for the establishment of "a powerful army and navy" against the "Sino-Japanese coalition," and so on.

War?

Capitalism is repeating the impasses of the first phase of finance capital hegemony, although less dramatically for the moment: it has shown itself incapable of adjusting its frontiers (decreases in valorization) or, to put it more precisely, it displaces them, as in the current crisis, but by multiplying and aggravating its impasses. At the start of the last century, the same dynamic led to war. For French socialists (Jean Jaurès, Jules Guesde) and German social-democrats (Kautsky), globalization was likely to create transnational corporations that would promote and conserve peace. A speech Jaurès gave at the National Assembly in December 1911 merits attention. The internationalization of the economy, he argues, is at work "beyond the boundaries of race and beyond the boundaries of trade" among "the great corporations of industrial and finance capital. [...] The power of the big banks towers above, coordinating capital, linking up business interests," and "in this way capitalist solidarity has begun, a formidable force when directed by inferior interests but which, when inspired by the common will of peoples, can become at certain moments a guarantee of peace."[31] In a situation where economic activities are tightly integrated, war is supposed to be economic nonsense. Lenin quite vigorously denounced such illusions, such "opportunism," affirming on the contrary that, from capital's point of view, destruction is necessary to the protection of property. We have the confirmation right before our eyes.

When the economic boom of the so-called "new economy" came, economists and experts pushed the lunacy still further. It was no longer war that was strictly out of the question but crises as well. It was the total victory of capital over communism and of capital over itself. In reality, only neoliberals' use of Keynesian mechanisms of state (monetary and social) intervention enabled capitalism to avoid a crisis like that of 1929. But if such a crisis seems to have been postponed, the remedies proposed in order to exit the crisis serve only to reproduce in a more expansive way the conditions that triggered it: after the private real-estate and financial markets demonstrated their capacity for destruction, our elites decided to subject as many public services as possible to privatization (in Spain they even privatized blood donations!). The "reform" of the job market, cuts in social spending, and the use of taxes as a tool for redistributing income to the advantage of capital continue to worsen inequalities (class differences). Only the pace has changed—it has sped up.

The growth that is supposed to result from "structural reforms" is exactly the same as that which caused the crisis, for growth is programmed to perpetuate the M–M' logic and its disequilibriums, its income and property inequalities, the impoverishment of the majority of the population and the increasing wealth of a minority. The crisis has continued since the 1970s, yet over the last forty years the wealth of Western countries has doubled. We are two times richer, but money is short everywhere except on the stock market, in tax havens, the bottom lines of multinationals, and the bank accounts of a tiny portion of the population.

The situation is obviously very different from that of Lenin's time and in certain ways more extreme. "What means other than war could there be *under capitalism* to overcome the disparity between the development of productive forces and the accumulation of capital on the one side, and the division of colonies and spheres of influence for finance capital on the other?"[32] Today the situation is still worse because the "disparity" is not economic, it does not only concern wage-earners, income, and patrimony. Capitalism produces "absolute" disparities.

Destruction is no longer temporarily confined to certain moments of the economic cycle. Since the end of the Second World War, the destructive side of capital has been "institutionalized" in the possibility for absolute destruction that has always loomed in each phase of the capitalist cycle: the atomic bomb, nuclear energy, and the ecological destruction of the planet. The infinite does not only govern production, consumption, and appropriation, so well represented by finance capital. The infinite is also the law of the destructive side of capital.

In the 1950s Günther Anders traced the contours of the new situation in which creative destruction and nuclear and ecological destruction combine. But, he writes, the production of the world by capital also contains

> its own alternative, the possibility of its interruption. [...] Even if this interruption does not take place tomorrow, it might take place the day after, in the generation of our great grandchildren or in the "seventh generation," because of what we do today. Since the effects of what we do today *persist*, we have already reached this future—

which means, pragmatically, that it is already present. It is as present, for example, as an enemy is "present," even when it appears absent.[33]

We do know one thing that Marx did not: every productive act of capital is also at the same time a destructive act. It is, therefore, not only "man" and "nature" but also science and technique that must be "freed" from the hold of capital and labor. Are we capable of making a political break with such "absolute" madness? I believe that events will force our hand. This is at least our (my) last bit of hope.

CONCLUSIONS FOR A BEGINNING:

THE REFUSAL OF WORK

The situation: Completely privatized, pacified, and colonized, public space intermittently returns to life only when struggles open up islands of non-communication, of non-response, of non-speech, of refusal of the "general mobilization," the only things capable of creating the conditions for new possibilities of expression, new words, and democratic practices.

The workers' strike was effective not only because it blocked the valorization of capital, but also because it made workers "equal" by releasing them from the division of labor in which they had been assigned different and competing places and functions.

We must recapture these conditions, arrest valorization, desert the flux of communication/consumption/production, and in this way recover equality, the basis of political organization. In order for subjectivation to emerge, we do not need to accelerate but to slow down. We need "time," but a time of rupture, a time that arrests the "general mobilization," a time that suspends apparatuses of exploitation and domination—an "idle time."

Laziness: With a touch of irony, in homage to Paul Lafarge and his refutation of the "dogma of work," I call "laziness" political action that at once refuses and eludes the roles, functions, and significations of the social division of labor and, in so doing, creates new possibilities. Why bring back laziness from the limbo to which the workers' movement had relegated it? Because it allows us to think and to practice the "refusal of work" starting from an ethical-political principle that will perhaps lead us out of the enchanted circle of production, productivity, and producers ("we are the true producers!"). Labor, production, and producers have been at once the strength and the weakness of the communist tradition. But was it supposed to be emancipation from work or through work? The ambiguity has never been cleared up. We must not take labor, whatever it may be, as our starting point but always the refusal of work.

Socialism: Artists alone have followed through on Kazimir Malevich's *The Right to Be Lazy*. In his small book *Laziness: The Real Truth of Mankind*, he denounces socialism, which seeks to ensure that "all of humanity follows a single laborious path and that no inactive person remains."[1] This is the actual program of today's ultraliberal European Commission. Malevich, writing during the first years of the Russian Revolution, believes that labor leads to laziness whereas if we start with labor, we always end up with labor (or, worse still, employment).

The refusal of work I: Lazy action is not "non-action" or "minimal action." It entails taking a position with respect to the conditions of existence in capitalist society. It expresses a subjective refusal that aims at the dominant power relation in capitalism: (wage) labor. "It's shameful we're still obliged to work simply to survive [...], obliged to work to exist—it really is a disgrace," said another artist, Marcel Duchamp,[2] who remained faithful his entire life to Lafargue's book. And the same is true today, despite cognitive capitalism, new technologies, "human capital," Facebook, Google, etc.

The refusal of work does not only concern workers; it specifically and above all means not wanting to be assigned a function, a role, and an identity predetermined in and by the social division of labor. From this perspective, factory worker, artist, woman, and "cognitive worker" are exactly the same thing—assignations. With or without a direct boss, all are caught up in relations of exploitation and domination. Production for the market subjects them all in different ways to economic and subjective impoverishment, to the expropriation, normalization, and standardization of their knowledge, their skills, and their lives.

The refusal of work II: Neoliberalism was constructed in response to the workers' refusal to work on the assembly lines of major industry. It promised self-realization through work based on individual enterprise, liberty by virtue of personalized consumption, and socialization assured by generalized connectivity. These promises implied certain things that would go unsaid but have been discovered little by little: on the one hand, new forms of subjection and enslavement and, on the other, precariousness, poverty, individualization, and inequality. They have revealed their true nature in the creation of the indebted man, in recession, in demands of sacrifice, in the imposition of austerity and the authoritarianism of permanent crisis.

The revolts rattling capitalism since 2007 contain a new radicality, because they reveal at once a refusal to work according to the rules of "human capital," a refusal to work as a consumer, communicator, user, or unemployed person, and a refusal of normalized gender identities, in other words, a refusal of a range of techniques of governmentality, those of valorization and those of subjection/enslavement.

The refusal of work III: We must emphasize the "refusal" as much as "work," and perhaps still more the first, for if work has changed, the subjective rupture that expresses refusal remains indispensable to defining political action. Refusal interrupts the course of time (and history), establishing a before and after that affect subjectivity first of all. Between this before and after (May '68), subjectivities are made and unmade.

Forced labor: Since the dawn of humanity, the generations that have sacrificed the most time at work are those that have had the misfortune of being born under capital. Every increase in productivity, every discovery or invention of science and technique, instead of freeing up time, has chained humanity more vigorously to capital, since it is the multiplicity of temporalities that has been transformed into profit. The contemporary refusal of work more profoundly undermines capital than the factory workers' refusal ever could, because exploitation affects society as a whole and subjectivity in all its dimensions. What is at stake is the "anthropology" of modernity (the subject, the individual, freedom, universality—all, of course, in the masculine).

Between speed and immobility: These new modalities of the refusal of work are specific forms of action that, between the bad infinity of capitalist accumulation and the unchanging stability of traditional societies, between the accelerated speed of money flows and the frustrating repetition of work, consumption, and communication, disclose the temporality of the "possible," the loose expansive time of a present of multiple durations, another space-time developing at the greatest speed and at the slowest. This "between" time must be transformed into a time of organization with the aid of machines and technology. No room for technophobia, then, because the greatest speed as well as the slowest are indeed the speeds of machines once freed from the hold of valorization.[3]

Like the strike, refusal operates a suspension of the generalized mobilization decreed by capital; it steers chronological time off track and reveals other movements, speeds, and rhythms. For Deleuze, access to this temporality is the privilege of the "seer," while for Duchamp it is that of the lazy person. How can these conceptual and existential figures be transformed into political ones?

Time: We need another way of living time. If time is money for the capitalist, for the lazy person and the seer "capital is time." Capital is in the process of repossessing all the temporalities that the worker's refusal of work had "liberated." The new struggle over time that is taking shape goes hand in hand with the appropriation of accumulated social wealth. To re-transform money into available time, to transform wealth into possibility, not only struggle but also new processes of subjectivation are needed.

Masculine/feminine: "Lazy" action operates disidentification. Its introduction into a world organized around activity undermines identities themselves, especially gender identities. Since antiquity, activity (sexual, political, productive) has been identified with men. Women, on the other hand, have been inactivity and passivity incarnate. Greek democracy celebrated political action as a domain exclusively reserved for men. The "democratization of slavery" carried out by capitalism has put at its center, not political action, but production. Nonetheless, producers are still men and work remains a manifestation of virility. The distinction between (masculine) activity and (feminine) inactivity can be found in the social sciences like psychoanalysis that came to prominence in the late-nineteenth and early-twentieth centuries. For Freud, activity is represented by daddy's dick, so if you do not have one, things can get tricky since something really is lacking. Lazy action suspends identities and opens up new becomings. It collapses the virility of action and work and puts into question the domination of women and nature.

Perception and sense: Although their purpose is to produce money, the operations of capital have more than economic effects. Capital endows us with perception and a certain sensibility because to perceive and to feel are functions of action. We see and we feel what is necessary to accomplish an action. To change perception and our ways of feeling, we must change our way of acting, in other words, in the final analysis, our way of living. Lazy action is the exact opposite of the purpose-driven action of capitalist production, for which the end (money) is everything and the process nothing. The latter literally would not exist if it did not produce money. The refusal of work, on the other hand, is entirely invested in the process, in the development, in the collective modalities of singularization.

Laziness and unemployment: The unemployed person is not "lazy," for unemployment is and has always been one of capital's temporalities. The unemployed person might become lazy, but as for anyone else, he does so at the price of work on the self, of a radical change of perspective with respect to the self, others, and the world.

Life: That capital exploits life does not mean that life coincides with capital. It is always possible to distinguish life from work, just as among wage-earners one can distinguish work from the worker. Even with the artist, who might be considered the prototype of human capital, one can distinguish artwork from life. "I wanted to use painting, to use art, as a way of establishing a *modus vivendi*, kind of a way of understanding life, in other words, probably to try to make life itself a work of art instead of spending my life making works of art in the form of paintings [...]. The important thing is to live and have a certain comportment. This comportment determines the paintings I've made, the puns I've made, and everything I've done, in public in any case" (Duchamp).[4] This separation is always possible because the subjectivation process is something that always remains a task to be undertaken. With the crisis, the belief in neoliberalism, a belief coerced by the promise that everyone could create an "authentic" life for themselves, is now falling apart. What does it mean to conceive, rather than an individual life, collective life as a work of art?

The democratic process: It is not the cognitive or the immaterial or any other definition derived from production that qualifies political action; it is refusal and the capacity to create new possibilities and escape the categories, identities, and roles of the *social* division of labor. Refusal and its potential for political action are not directly deducible from "labor," from the roles and functions to which we are assigned.[5] Refusal implies an action that renounces the division of labor and opens to what is impossible within that division. Lazy action requires no virtuosity, no specialized skill, whether cognitive or professional. Anyone can practice it.

But in what way might it become the engine of the collective process of organizing? The temporality of organization is specific. My most recent political experience with La Coordination des Intermittents et Précaires d'Île-de-France[6] taught me that a democratic process based on an interruption, on demobilization, takes time, a lot of time, enough to discover that subjective forces, their production, organization, and recomposition, are indeed possible. The speed and simplifications of democratic centralism or those of the social networks listed on the stock market cannot solve the problem. The condition for using and organizing the heterogeneous speeds that struggle demands is to develop that which is involved in the non-movement of demobilization.

The war machine: And yet the dualisms of capital must be undone. Without the ability to establish and maintain relations of power, it is impossible to exploit the implications and singularities contained in the refusal of work. The refusal of work means nothing else. It does not refer to the party or the state as it does among theorists of factory workers' refusal. It is difficult to conceive a becoming-party or becoming-state of feminist (or precarious worker) movements, which have, on the contrary, made other strategic choices: to stick with the refusal of work and its political potential by exploiting all its possibilities. The need to discover, produce, and reconstitute temporalities, heterogeneous subjectivities and their institutions, requires that we continually seek to elude the techniques of subjection and enslavement deployed by governmentality.

Notes

Introductory Glossary

1. Gilles Deleuze, lecture at Vincennes, December 17, 1971. Available at: http://www.webdeleuze.com/php/texte.php?cle=118& groupe=Anti%20Oedipe%20et%20Mille%20Plateaux&langue=1.

2. Nietzsche helps us to grasp the meaning of the untimely that political refusal implies, without leaving history and its relations of power and significations: "What deed would man be capable of if he had not first entered into that vaporous region of the unhistorical?" (*Untimely Meditations*, trans. R. J. Hollingdale [Cambridge: Cambridge University Press, 2007], 64). History is not made by those who participate in or alter it but by those who oppose its course.

1. Profit, Rent, Taxes: Three Apparatuses of Capture

1. The passage is quoted by Carl Schmitt in a footnote to the French translation of his essay "Nehmen/Teilen/Weiden," "Prendre/ partager/paître" (Appropriation/Distribution/ Production), *La guerre civile mondiale*, trans. Céline Jouin (Maisons-Alfort, France: Éditions Ère, 2007), 63. The passage is not included in the English translation of Schmitt's essay. The footnote in which Marx cites Goethe is taken from Karl Marx, *Oeuvres complètes*, vol. 1 (Paris: Gallimard, 1963). Translator's note.

2. National Institute of Statistics and Economic Studies.

3. I refer here to the "three-headed" apparatus of *A Thousand Plateaus* (rent, profit, taxation), substituting land rent for financial rent. Gilles Deleuze and Félix Guattari, trans. Brian Massumi (Minneapolis: University of Minnesota Press, 2005), 443–444.

4. What economics fails to see is the political origin of its object of study: "Like Charlemagne, the Ottonian Emperors wanted to control commercial operations and thereby bring them within a stable political framework. Accordingly they established markets in a land that knew little of such institutions. From extant documents we know of twenty-nine of these foundations belonging to the period 936–1002." "The creation of a *mercatus* would be accompanied by that of a mint, so that any site set aside for commercial dealings might regularly be supplied with coins. The Emperor granted these minting rights to local potentates: counts, bishops, and moneyers." Georges Duby, *The Early Growth of the European Economy*, trans. Howard B. Clarke (Ithaca, New York: Cornell University Press, 1974), 132, 134.

5. *Op. cit.*, 422.

6. Gilles Deleuze and Félix Guattari, *Anti-Oedipus*, trans. Robert Hurley, Mark Seem, and Helen R. Lane (Minneapolis: University of Minnesota Press, 2000), 197.

7. Gilles Deleuze and Félix Guattari, *A Thousand Plateaus*, *op. cit.*, 422.

8. Gilles Deleuze and Félix Guattari, *Anti-Oedipus*, *op. cit.*

9. The significance and scope of taxation are less evident in income taxes than in indirect taxes, not only because the latter are not progressive and represent the largest share of taxes the state collects, but also because they make up a portion of the cost of goods determined independently of the market. Market prices are a part of this non-economic political foundation.

10. Over the last four years Italy (under Berlusconi and Monti), the third largest European economy, has been subject to "reforms

designed to put accounts in order." These have exacted 329.5 billion euros from the Italian population, 55% through new taxes.

11. Gilles Deleuze and Félix Guattari, *A Thousand Plateaus, op. cit.*, 442.

12. *Ibid.*

13. Carl Schmitt, "The Legal World Revolution," trans. G. L. Ulmen, *Telos* 72 (Summer 1987): 79. The adage literally means "Whose realm, his religion." In Schmitt's new formulation, industry or the economy replaces power.

14. Carl Schmitt, *The* Nomos *of the Earth*, trans. G. L. Ulmen (New York: Telos Press, 2003), 334.

15. Carl Schmitt, "The Legal World Revolution," *op. cit.*, 80.

16. Carl Schmitt, *The* Nomos *of the Earth, op. cit.*, 327.

17. *Ibid.*, 334.

18. Carl Schmitt, "Prendre/partager/paître," *La guerre civile mondiale, op. cit.*, 64.

19. Carl Schmitt, *The* Nomos *of the Earth, op. cit.*, 331.

20. Carl Schmitt, "The Legal World Revolution," *op. cit.*

21. Denis Kessler, the second in command of the largest French employers' union (Mouvement des entreprises de France), himself spoke of "spoils" in a text attesting to his deference to finance and the insurance industry: businesses must "reincorporate" the social programs they had externalized during Fordism, when they delegated them to the state. He estimated that the spoils to be had in public spending came to 2.6 billion francs [396 million euros] for the service industry in 1999. The privatization of public insurance, the individualization of social policy, and the drive to make social protections an extension of business are at the heart of employers'

neoliberal project. "L'avenir de la protection sociale," *Commentaire* 87:22 (fall 1999): 619–632.

22. Carl Schmitt, *The* Nomos *of the Earth, op. cit.*, 332.

23. Carl Schmitt, "State Ethics and the Pluralist State," in *Weimar: A Jurisprudence of Crisis*, trans. Belinda Cooper (Berkeley: University of California Press, 2000), 312.

24. Quoted in Carl Schmitt, *The* Nomos *of the Earth, op. cit.*, 332–333.

25. Carl Schmitt, *The* Nomos *of the Earth, op. cit.*, 347.

2. The American University: A Model of the Debt Society

1. Gilles Dostaler and Bernard Maris, *Capitalisme et pulsion de mort* (Paris: Albin Michel, 2009), 98.

2. Marcel Hénaff, *The Price of Truth*, trans. Jean-Louis Morhange (Stanford: Stanford University Press, 2010), 20.

3. Jean-Pierre Dupuy, *Le sacrifice et l'envie: Le libéralisme aux prises avec la justice sociale* (Paris: Calmann-Lévy, 1996).

4. The Federal Reserve's study demonstrates the trend: 32% of debtors are forty years old or more and 5% are sixty years old or more. In 2010, nearly one American household in five (19%) had a student loan to repay, that is, more than twice as many as twenty years ago and 15% more than in 2007.

5. The Fed notes that the percentage of student debtors who are in default (8.69% in the first quarter) is higher than that for real estate and car loans, a percentage that is no doubt an underestimate.

6. As Alan Greenspan, the former Federal Reserve chairman from 1987 to 2006, used to say, a home functions like a bank, because its price, by constantly rising, allows you to open infinite new lines of debt/credit.

7. Although financial transactions are anonymous, commercial transactions are increasingly not anonymous. The number of purchases made with credit cards has risen exponentially, necessitating electronic identities in order for them to be carried out. The bank can follow your purchases, marketing companies your lifestyle, etc., in real time. The picture we have of exchange (and even of credit) between two free and equal individuals, a transaction founded on trust, is here in fact undermined, since exchange is mediated by technical and institutional systems, banks and their payment system. Instead of conserving anonymity, the "market" keeps us under constant surveillance.

8. Students' transformation into a "personal enterprise" presents no advantages whatsoever. Although compelled to behave like a business, they cannot go bankrupt because American law prohibits it. A bill in the Senate has proposed giving to indebted current and former university students the right to declare bankruptcy, as is already the case for all other borrowers.

9. A. J. Haesler, *Sociologie de l'argent et post-modernité* (Geneva: Droz, 1995), 255.

10. Georg Simmel has best described the nature of exchange-money and the freedom it involves: "In contrast to the simple taking-away or gift, in which the purely subjective impulse is enjoyed, exchange presupposes [...] an objective appraisal, consideration, mutual acknowledgment, a restraint of direct subjective desire," *The Philosophy of Money*, trans. Tom Bottomore and David Frisby (New York: Routledge, 2011), 314. By eliminating the personal, money increases the freedom of the individual, "since it makes possible relationships between people but leaves them personally undisturbed" (327). On the other hand, credit and its operations and, therefore, money as capital are completely absent except as practiced by "men of distinction": "It is not necessary to be a gentleman in order to obtain credit, but rather that whoever demands credit is a gentleman" (520). Alas, this courtly conception of "credit" ignores not only capitalist credit but capitalism itself.

11. *Desert Islands and Other Texts, 1953–1974*, trans. Michael Taomina (Los Angeles: Semiotext(e), 2002), 263. [trans. modified]

12. *Ibid.*, 262.

13. *Anti-Oedipus*, trans. Robert Hurley, Mark Seem, and Helen R. Lane (Minneapolis: University of Minnesota Press, 1983), 230.

14. Michel Aglietta and André Orléan, *La monnaie souveraine* (Paris: Odile Jacob, 1998), 21. For another conception of the "debt of the living," see Elettra Stimilli, *Il debito del vivente* (Macerata: Quodlibet, 2011).

15. Aglietta and Orléan, *op. cit.*, 21.

16. "The association of reactive forces is thus accompanied by a transformation of debt; this becomes a debt toward 'divinity,' toward 'society,' toward 'the State,' toward reactive instances. [...] Debt loses the active character by virtue of which it took part in man's liberation: in its new form it is inexhaustible, *unpayable*. [...] Debt becomes the relation of a debtor who will never finish paying to a creditor who will never finish using up the interest on the debt: 'Debt toward the divinity.'" Gilles Deleuze, *Nietzsche and Philosophy*, trans. Hugh Tomlinson (New York: Continuum, 1986), 141–142.

17. Gilles Deleuze and Félix Guattari, *Anti-Oedipus, op. cit.*, 197.

18. René Girard, *Violence and the Sacred*, trans. Patrick Gregory (Baltimore: The Johns Hopkins University Press, 1977), 299–300.

19. Alain Testart, *Des dons et des dieux* (Paris: Armand Colin, 1993), 29.

20. Eduardo Viveiros de Castro, *Métaphysiques cannibales*, trans. Oiara Bonilla (Paris: Presses Universitaires de France, 2009), 110.

21. *Ibid.*, 123.

22. *Ibid.*, 128.

23. David Graeber, *Debt: The First 5,000 Years* (Brooklyn: Melville House, 2011).

24. Even in archaic societies, reciprocity does not mean equilibrium, equity, or symmetry, contrary to what Graeber believes: "Gifts can be reciprocal, but even that does not make exchange a less violent event: the whole purpose of the act of giving is to force one's partner to act, to force a gesture out of him, to provoke a response—in short, to steal his soul (the alliance as a reciprocal theft of souls). In this sense, there is no social act that is not an 'exchange of gifts,' for no act is social except as an action upon an action, a reaction upon a reaction. Reciprocity here simply means recursivity. No hint of sociability, and still less of altruism. Life is theft." Eduardo Viveiros de Castro, *Métaphysiques cannibales, op. cit.*, 139.

25. Friedrich Nietzsche, *On the Genealogy of Morals*, trans. Walter Kaufman and R. J. Hollingdale (New York: Vintage Books, 1989), 56, 55.

26. *Ibid.*, 20.

27. Gilles Deleuze and Félix Guattari, *Anti-Oedipus, op. cit.*, 185.

28. *Ibid.*, 144.

29. Friedrich Nietzsche, *On the Genealogy of Morals, op. cit.*, 58.

30. *Ibid.*, 86.

31. *Ibid.*, 91.

32. The German word Kafka uses, "Verschleppung," also has a legal meaning, as the term "atermoiement" does in French and "moratorium" in English. The latter refer even more specifically to the creditor-debtor relation, to the period a creditor authorizes a debtor to postpone payment.

33. Gilles Deleuze, "Postscript on the Societies of Control," *October* 59 (Winter 1992): 4.

3. Critique of Governmentality I: Does Liberal Governmentality Exist? Has It Ever Existed?

1. Gilles Deleuze, "Nature des flux," lecture at Vincennes, December 14, 1971. Available at: http://www.webdeleuze.com/php/texte.php?cle=118&groupe=Anti%20Oedipe%20et%20Mille%20Plateaux&langue=1.

2, Michel Foucault, *Security, Territory, Population*, trans. Graham Burchell (New York: Palgrave MacMillan, 2007), 143.

3. *Ibid.*, 319.

4. *Anti-Oedipus*, trans. Robert Hurley, Mark Seem, and Helen R. Lane (Minneapolis: University of Minnesota Press, 1983), 253.

5. *Ibid.*

6. Michel Foucault, *The Birth of Biopolitics*, trans. Graham Burchell (New York: Palgrave Macmillan, 2008), 322.

7. *Ibid.*, 21.

8. Gilles Deleuze and Félix Guattari, *Anti-Oedipus, op. cit.*, 252.

9. The Italian theory of the "autonomy of the political" put forward by Mario Tronti centers on a qualitative leap of the working class, which, in order to conclude the revolutionary process, must "make itself a state." Making itself a state within the welfare state means quite simply becoming an articulation of "capital," becoming "variable capital" within the state, that is, becoming what the working class had refused to do within the factory. All the struggles that have taken place, and especially those over "income" and "services" during the 1970s, considered the welfare state, its governmentality and control of body, soul, and life, their "enemy."

10. Michael Foucault, *The Birth of Biopolitics*, trans. Graham Burchell (New York: Palgrave Macmillan, 2008), 86–87.

11. *Ibid.*, 84.

12. *Ibid.*

13. *Ibid.*, 86.

14. *Ibid.*, 321.

15. *Ibid.*, 140.

16. *Ibid.*, 240.

17. *Ibid.*, 241.

18. *Ibid.*, 242.

19. *Ibid.*

20. *Ibid.*, 225.

21. *Ibid.*, 167.

22. *Ibid.*, 175.

23. *Ibid.*, 321.

24. *Ibid.*, 319.

25. André Orléan, *Le pouvoir de la finance* (Paris: Odile Jacob, 1999), 249.

26. There is a still more profound difference between the two types of debt because political debt derives directly from "primitive debt," the original debt of individuals toward ancestors and the gods. Original debt is not a bilateral relationship as it is in contemporary finance "but a social relationship defining the membership of the individual in the community" (*see* Michel Aglietta and André Orléan, *La Monnaie souveraine* [Paris: Odile Jacob, 1998]). Today "life debt" and the sanctity that goes along with it are taken

up by the state such that original sin (or lack, according to a secularized, psychoanalytic reading) is replaced by debt. For a radically different interpretation of how the state assumes the "finite debt" of archaic societies (or empires) and the latter's transformation into "infinite debt," see the genealogy of debt Deleuze and Guattari delineate and my summary in *The Making of the Indebted Man*, trans. Joshua David Jordan (Los Angeles: Semiotext(e), 2012).

27. André Orléan, *Le pouvoir de la finance, op. cit.*, 245.

28. Michel Aglietta and André Orléan, *La monnaie entre violence et confiance* (Paris: Odile Jacob, 2002), 116.

29. Michel Aglietta and André Orléan, *La monnaie souveraine, op. cit.*, 11.

30. André Orléan, *Le pouvoir de la finance, op. cit.*, 246.

31. Heterodox theory wavers in its definition of private money between money as means of payment, of measurement and accumulation (the functions of money of market societies), and money as capital. In the end, it reduces the latter, specifically capitalist money, to market functions. The capitalist relation is introduced after the commodity and currency, whereas in reality the capitalist relation comes first. Money as capital drives the process. It must necessarily be at the beginning.

32. In the heterodox theory of money we find another, surprising opposition used to explain the problematic duality of monetary circuits, one derived from Durkheim's "republican" sociology: sovereign money as the expression of the collective and economic money as the expression of the individual. This attempt to find some mediation to the conflict in the "social" sphere is destined to fail because, as we learn from Carl Schmitt and still more from the "liberal" management of the crisis, the social, like the state, like institutions, etc., is traversed by class struggle.

33. David Graeber, *Debt: The First 5,000 Years* (Brooklyn: Melville House, 2011).

34. Karl Marx, *Grundrisse*, trans. Martin Nicolaus (New York: Penguin, 1973), 367.

35. Michel Aglietta and André Orléan, *La monnaie souveraine, op. cit.*, 372.

36. *Ibid.*, 373. Orléan makes an interesting point when he asserts that the only time that sovereign money functions like "capital" is when it finances the Treasury, that is, when it makes decisions on social spending and state investments by functioning as the power to prescribe and control social production. This is precisely what Europe, more liberal than America, has prohibited.

37. *Ibid.*, 382.

38. *Ibid.*, p. 380.

4. Critique of Governmentality II: Capital and the Capitalism of Flows

1. Michel Foucault, *The Birth of Biopolitics*, trans. Graham Burchell (New York: Palgrave MacMillan, 2008), 174.

2. *Ibid.*, 165.

3. *Ibid.*, 167.

4. *Ibid.*, 162.

5. *Ibid.*, 164.

6. Félix Guattari, "Sepulchre for an Oedipus Complex," *Molecular Revolution*, trans. Rosemary Sheed (New York: Penguin, 1984), 6–10.

7. Félix Guattari, "The Group and the Person," *ibid.*, 30.

8. *Ibid.*, 34.

9. Gilles Deleuze, lecture at Vincennes, December, 21, 1971. Available at: http://www.webdeleuze.com/php/texte.php?cle=121& groupe=Anti%20Oedipe%20et%20Mille%20Plateaux&langue=1.

10. Gilles Deleuze and Félix Guattari, *Anti-Oedipus*, trans. Robert Hurley (Minneapolis: University of Minnesota Press, 1983), 230.

11. See Chapter 3 for the historical development of this hegemony.

12. "The capitalist revolution attacks all previous territorialities; it dislocates rural, provincial, and corporate communities; it deterritorializes holidays, religions, music, traditional icons; it 'colonizes' not only former aristocracies but also all the marginal or nomadic strata of society." Félix Guattari, *Lignes de fuite* (La Tour d'Aigues, France: De l'Aube, 2011), 54.

13. Since securities can be exchanged, current and future investment flows constitute a market in which stock-market "speculation" takes place. But to believe that it is exchange between traders that determines the laws of capital is to confuse cause and effect— what economists carelessly did when thinking that commodity exchange determines the laws of the economy.

14. G. Deleuze and F. Guattari, *A Thousand Plateaus*, trans. Brian Massumi (Minneapolis: University of Minnesota Press, 1987), 461.

15. In the debt economy, one mustn't think of the rentier as a nineteenth-century bourgeois who "gets rich in his sleep." Among rentiers one must also and necessarily include the enterprise which, while it works for rentiers, also shares with other rentiers a portion of the social surplus value captured by finance.

16. Gilles Deleuze, lecture at Vincennes, February 22, 1972. Available at: http://www.webdeleuze.com/php/texte.php?cle=158 &groupe=Anti+Oedipe+et+Mille+Plateaux&langue=1.

17. Gilles Deleuze and Félix Guattari, *A Thousand Plateaus, op. cit.*, 461. From the start, scientific axiomatics is not a simple logical-deductive system but a politics, the management of conflict, a

struggle for control over semiotic flows, scientific statements and their assemblages.

18. *Ibid.*, 454.

19. "[C]apitalism has from the beginning mobilized a force of deterritorialization infinitely surpassing the deterritorialization proper to the State" such that capitalism "is not at all territorial, even in its beginnings," *ibid.*, 453–454.

20. *Ibid.*, 456. The homogeneity and competition of capital have, "In order to be effectuated, […] always required there to be a new force and a new law of State," *ibid.*, 455. The state plays the role of indispensable economic actor because it contributes to the realization of surplus value by regulating "effective demand." From the economic point of view, the state, despite what liberals think, does not take surplus value from private enterprise but rather pushes the capitalist economy to its maximum output. The limits which capital always confronts in its insatiable desire for valorization could not be moved without state intervention.

21. Once integrated into the state, the workers' movement assured, until the 1970s, the most durable reterritorialization and the most stable subjections that capitalism has ever known, by providing "compensatory territories," subjects, and socialist values which were added to those of the state in order to ensure the relations of capital.

22. Gilles Deleuze and Félix Guattari, *Anti-Oedipus, op. cit.*, 251–252.

23. The notion of the cybernetic machine that Hayek uses to explain the market involves "feedback loops" based on a concept of totalization that the machine is supposed to master all by itself. The cybernetic machine functions via inputs and outputs whose purpose is to make it work "according to the principle of eternal return." Yet the machine always depends on entities external to it, it is always in dialogue with alterities. The machine stands at the junction of a multiplicity of universes (technological, diagrammatic,

industrial, imaginary, political, economic) that cannot be reduced or restricted to the structural conditions of the cybernetic machine. It would be better to situate the machine, as Leroi-Gourhan does with the tool, within its social, human, and bodily environment and within cultural, theoretical, political, and economic relations. If the essence of the digital machine is not decentered toward its "exterior," a reductive vision of the machine results. It is therefore necessary to carry out a decentering of the essence of machinism from its "visible part to its incorporeal part" (see Félix Guattari, "Qu'est-ce que l'écosophie," January, 1991. Available at: http://www.webdeleuze.com/php/texte.php?cle=90&groupe=Bibliographie%20et%20mondes%20in%E9dits&langue=1).

24. Michel Foucault, "La sécurité et l'État," in *Dits et Ecrits*, vol. 3 (Paris: Gallimard, 1994), 386.

25. Frédéric Gros, *Le principe sécurité* (Paris: Gallimard, 2012), 211.

26 This watered-down conception of techniques of security power is quite widespread among scholars and at times becomes so benign that it contrasts starkly with how these techniques actually function. "Much more than in relations with authority, it is through the play of soft normalization that the transformations of representations and behaviors take place. Better: it is often the law itself that provides for the transfer of legitimacy that allows individuals themselves to decide the best way to self-govern, the best way to protect their health, control reproduction, construct their lives, choose their death. The relation of the self to the self and of the self to others, grounded in self-examination and a respect for differences, becomes the standard of good conduct. To govern means ensuring that individuals govern themselves in the very best way they can." Didier Fassin and Dominique Memmi, "Le gouvernement de la vie, mode d'emploi," in *Le gouvernement des corps* (Paris: Editions de l'EHESS. 2004).

27. Michel Foucault, *La société punitive* (Paris: Gallimard/Seuil, 2013), 33. The same thing happens with money. In his lectures on neoliberalism, *The Birth of Biopolitics*, Foucault does not return to the analysis of money developed in his 1970–1971 *Lectures on the*

Will to Know in which he makes it the foundation of power and the economy.

28. *Ibid.*

29. Michel Foucault, *Society Must Be Defended*, trans. David Macey (New York: Picador, 2003), 132.

30. *Ibid.*, 133, 132.

31. *Ibid.*, 161.

32. Félix Guattari, "De la production de subjectivité," *Chimères* 4 (Winter 1987).

33. Gilles Deleuze, "Nature des flux," lecture at Vincennes, December 14, 1971. Available at: http://www.webdeleuze.com/ php/texte.php?cle=118&groupe=Anti%20Oedipe%20et%20Mille %20Plateaux&langue=1.

5. Critique of Governmentality III: Who Governs Whom, What, and How?

1. Michel Foucault, *Security, Territory, Population*, trans. Graham Burchell (New York: Palgrave Macmillan, 2007), 120.

2. In Foucault's lectures we find references to the new apparatuses of governmentality: "Today [...] full employment of time is assured through leisure activities, entertainment, consumption, which entails reconstituting the full employment of time that was in the nineteenth century one of the primary concerns of capitalism." *La société punitive* (Paris: Gallimard/Seuil, 2013), 216. In disciplinary societies the apparatuses of production and control of subjectivity are often multiplied on the initiative of private institutions. Foucault remarks that they "take the state structure as a model; they are little states," *ibid.*, 214. On the other hand, the model today comes from private enterprise, even for the state.

3. Karl Marx, *Grundrisse*, trans. Martin Nicolaus (New York: Penguin, 1973), 694.

4. The same paradigm is present in a different form among liberals like Hayek, one founded on the subject/object dichotomy. Subjects' actions, dictated by individual self-interest, are coordinated automatically, bringing to life a new "objective" entity constituting, by way of their actions, a "subjectless" process. Individuals act but the result of their actions is not the project of a will, the "design of consciousness." The market is a "spontaneous order" which no will has intended and no consciousness anticipated. The automaton is a metaphor for the spontaneous order of the market guaranteeing both the autonomy of the individual and the autonomy of the social sphere. Just as mysteriously as Marxian fetishism, we move from the order of the subject to the order of the object. The difference has to do with judgment, an alienating mechanism for Marx, for Hayek one that frees us from personal servitude. The same movement can be found in various forms in sociology's concept of "the social." To explain it, Hayek uses the metaphor of the cybernetic automaton he borrows from Von Neumann, which supposedly solves the paradox of an automaton over which its human inventor has no control. Hayek argues that the automaton belongs to an order of entities supposedly more complex than the individual. It seems to me, however, that if we stick to the modern subject/object paradigm, if we cannot situate "objectivity" and "subjectivity" differently, both in the human and in the non-human, an aporia always results.

5. The maximization of this process is exemplified in the behavior expected of the private contractor, the free-lancer, but also in that of the precarious worker, the unemployed, and welfare recipients. Yet the truth is that the injunction to be a subject and thus to take the initiative and assume responsibility concerns everyone.

6. "The whole fabric of the capitalist world consists of this kind of flux of deterritorialized signs—money and economic signs [...]. Significations, social values (those one can interpret, that is) can be seen at the level of power formations, but, essentially, capitalism depends upon non-signifying machines. There is, for instance, no

meaning in the ups and downs of the stock market [...]. Capitalism gives each of us our particular role—doctor, child, teacher, man, woman, homosexual—and it is up to us to adapt ourselves to the system of signification arranged for each of us. But at the level of real power, it is never this type of role that is at issue; power does not have to be identified with the director or the minister—it operates in relationships of finance and force, and among different pressure groups. A-signifying machines do not recognize agents, individuals, roles or even clearly defined objects." Félix Guattari, *Molecular Revolution*, trans. Rosemary Sheed (New York: Penguin, 1984), 171–172.

7. The functions of money are not reducible to asignifying activity and manifest themselves through interaction with other semiotics: at the "symbolic" level, money functions like an imaginary subjection of the individual. His purchasing power is "remotely controlled not only in the domain of codes of social status but also in that of perceptual and sexual codes." The monetary economy "interacts constantly with the signifying encodings of language, in particular through the system of laws and regulations," Félix Guattari, *La Révolution moléculaire* (Paris: Union générale d'éditions, 1977), 295.

8. Pier Paolo Pasolini, *Écrits corsaires* (Paris: Flammarion, 1976), 79.

9. *Ibid.*, 95.

10. *Ibid.*, 93.

11. Félix Guattari, *Les Années d'hiver: 1980–1985* (Paris: Les Prairies Ordinaires, 2009), 163.

12. The indexation process even extends to and enables the measurement of erections. For example, in 1997 the multinational Pfizer, the Viagra manufacturer, developed the "International Index of Erectile Functions" (IIEF).

13. "Consumption for consumption's sake" and "production for production's sake" partake of different "moral" doctrines (and

modes of subjectivation). The first is the injunction to "enjoy," a morality of innocence and "expenditure," whereas the second is an injunction to "suffer," a morality of guilt and sacrifice. A third, the morality of debt, which is also an injunction to guilt and sacrifice, has emerged in a spectacular way in contemporary capitalism. The three moralities coexist and define three forms of the production of subjectivity which in the crisis interconnect in contradictory ways.

14. Michel Foucault, *The Birth of Biopolitics*, trans. Graham Burchell (New York: Palgrave MacMillan, 2008), 271.

15. Michel Foucault, *Security, Territory, Population, op. cit.*, 35.

16. Michel Foucault, *The Birth of Biopolitics, op. cit.*, 252.

17. Polling and opinion surveys produce statistical averages (the "French person," the "voter," and the "consumer" are always derived from statistical samples), whereas "profiles" end individualization, for in this case it is a matter of stockpiling the electronic "traces" that constitute the data base out of which profiles are constructed.

18. According to Guattari, capitalism produces subjective proto-types in the same way as it manufactures automobile prototypes.

19. Foucault seems to adopt an overly benign conception of these techniques. They do more than incite or solicit us to abandon the possibility of acting on our own. They are real instruments of police intervention into people's private lives. They establish generalized and universal police surveillance over every one of us.

20. Beatriz Preciado, *Testo Junkie*, trans. Bruce Benderson (New York: The Feminist Press, 2013).

21. The proportion of feminized cyprinid fish (chub)—a species particularly sensitive to the presence of estrogens in water—varies from 4% to 40%. We are talking about a phenomenon pervasive throughout Europe. The French government has launched a study to measure the feminization of these fish.

22. *Ibid.*, 158–159.

23. Gilbert Simondon, *Du mode d'existence des objets techniques* (Paris: Editions Aubier, 1989), 246.

24. Gilbert Simondon, *L'individuation à la lumière des notions de forme et d'information* (Grenoble: Editions Jérôme Millon, 2005), 524.

25. Norbert Wiener, *Cybernetics: or Control and Communication in the Animal and the Machine* (Cambridge: MIT Press, 1985), 161.

26. M. Foucault, *The Birth of Biopolitics, op. cit.* 260.

27. *Ibid.*, 259.

28. *Ibid.*, 259–260. More convincingly, Pier Paolo Pasolini had, some years before Foucault, identified the production and consumption of freedom and tolerance in a form of power more "subtle, clever, and complex" than that of disciplinary societies: "Personally, I do not believe that the current form of tolerance is real. It was decided 'on high': it is tolerance of the power of consumption, which requires an absolutely formal elasticity of 'existences' in order for everyone to become a good consumer […]. It is a false tolerance, certainly the prelude to a period of intolerance and racism," *Écrits corsaires, op. cit.*, 256. "The power of consumption has superseded the—let us say, liberal and progressive—demands for freedom and, by making them its own, has rendered them futile and changed their nature," *ibid.*, 145.

6. Rereading Lenin: The Past and Present of Finance Capital

1. We mention in passing that the history of capitalism, and notably the phase beginning during the late nineteenth century, sharply contradicts David Graeber's theory of long alternating periods of the hegemony of credit money followed by long periods of the hegemony of commodity money.

2. V. I. Lenin, *Imperialism, the Highest Stage of Capitalism*, in *Collected Works*, vol. 22, trans. Yuri Sdobnikov (London: Lawrence and Wishart, 1964), 207.

3. *Ibid.*, 268.

4. *Ibid.*, 220, 214.

5. Rudolf Hilferding, *Finance Capital*, trans. Morris Watnick and Sam Gordon (London: Routledge, 1981), 235.

6. *Ibid.*, 149.

7. *Ibid.*

8. V. I. Lenin, *op. cit.*, 206.

9. *Ibid.*, 238–239.

10. "[T]he 'rentier state' (Rentnerstaat), or usurer state, is coming into common use in the economic literature that deals with imperialism. The world has become divided into a handful of usurer states and a vast majority of debtor states," *ibid.*, 277.

11. *Ibid.*, 214–215.

12. See Sergio Bologna, *Banche e crisi* (Rome: Derive Approdi, 2013).

13. See Giovanni Arrighi, *Adam Smith in Beijing* (New York: Verso, 2009).

14. Mario Tronti, *Nous opéraïstes*, trans. Michel Valensi (Paris: L'Eclat, 2013), 20. Italian Operaism, with Tronti and Negri, is the only postwar Marxism to have returned to the Leninist concept of "collective capitalist" and sketched out a concept of "social surplus value," in an era of financialization a concept still more relevant today than in Fordism.

15. V. I. Lenin, *op. cit.*, 240.

16. Suzanne Berger, *Notre première mondialisation* (Paris: Seuil, 2003), 26.

17. V. I. Lenin, *op. cit.*, 278.

18. *Ibid.*, 254.

19. *Ibid.*, 277.

20. *Ibid.*, 290.

21. It should nonetheless be said that Lenin was right in the short term, for the new model of accumulation would be built on the ruins created by classical liberalism, that is, following thirty years of world wars, catastrophic economic crises, and bloody civil wars, and only once the danger of "communist" revolution had passed.

22. *Ibid.*, 241.

23. *Ibid.*, 282.

24. *Ibid.*, 281.

25. *Ibid.*, 279–280.

26. *Ibid.*, 280.

27. *Ibid.*, 282.

28. Suzanne Berger, *op. cit.*, 69.

29. V. I. Lenin, *op. cit.*, 303.

30. Gérard Duménil and Dominique Lévy, "Finance capitaliste: rapports de production et rapports de classe," in *La Finance capitaliste* (Paris: PUF, 2006), 144.

31. Quoted in Suzanne Berger, *op. cit.*

32. V. I. Lenin, *op. cit.*, 275–276.

33. Günther Anders, *L'Obsolescence de l'homme* (Paris: Éditions de l'encyclopédie des nuisances, 2002), 315.

Conclusions for a Beginning: The Refusal of Work

1. Kazimir Malevich, *La Paresse comme vérité effective de l'homme* (Paris: Allia, 2000), 14.

2. Quoted in Bernard Marcadé, *Laisser pisser les mérinos: la paresse de Marcel Duchamp* (Paris: L'Echoppe, 2006), 456.

3. I refer the reader to a book I wrote some time ago: *Videophilosophie* (Berlin: B-books, 2002).

4. Quoted in Bernard Marcadé, *Marcel Duchamp. La vie à credit* (Paris: Flammarion, 2007), 157.

5. Refusal has causes and goals, but the rupture it manifests emerges by way of a desire with no goal and with no cause. Its true cause is the rupture with causality (of the division of labor, production, and valorization); its goals do not preexist the rupture, which forces us to invent new ways of being and acting. While impossible in the order of causes (of the division of labor), rupture creates untimely possibilities, the condition for all new subjectivation.

6. Coordination of Intermittent and Precarious Workers of the Île-de-France. For a fuller discussion of this, see *Making of the Indebted Man*, trans. Joshua David Jordan (Los Angeles: Semiotext(e), 2012).

semiotext(e) intervention series